DANIEL BOONE

THE OPENING OF THE WILDERNESS

DANIEL BOONE

THE OPENING

OF THE WILDERNESS

★

by JOHN MASON BROWN

Illustrated by LEE J. AMES

When Daniel Boone goes by, at night,
The phantom deer arise
And all lost, wild America
Is burning in their eyes.

Rosemary and Stephen Vincent Benét
A BOOK OF AMERICANS

Landmark
BOOKS

RANDOM HOUSE · NEW YORK

To My Grandfather

JOHN MASON BROWN

Feeling as close to him as if I had known him, and wishing not only that I had but that I had known him as well as he knew Kentucky's early history.

CONTENTS

ACKNOWLEDGMENTS

I WOULD BE WORSE THAN AN INGRATE IF I LET THIS winnowing of incidents in the life of Daniel Boone and the opening of the wilderness appear without some statement, however inadequate, of my gratitude to those authorities who have done the real pioneering work. Although I have read many, many books on the subject, I am especially indebted to Douglas S. Freeman for the first volume of his *George Washington;* to my grandfather, John Mason Brown, for his *Oration Delivered on the Occasion of the Centennial Commemoration of the Battle of the Blue Licks;* to Reuben Gold Thwaites for his *Daniel Boone;* and to John Bakeless for his invaluable *Daniel Boone: Master of the Wilderness.* These men more than any others opened the Wilderness Road for me. In retelling Boone's story I have followed the trails blazed by them. Most particularly, I have been guided by Mr. Bakeless, whose meticulous scholarship, productive curiosity, and exhaustive research have brought to light hundreds of new details about Daniel and his times. His biography is the most complete account of Boone I know, a work as spirited as it is indispensable. I also wish to thank Rosemary Benét and Rinehart & Co., Inc. for permission to quote on the title page the poem about Daniel Boone by Rosemary and Stephen Vincent Benét from their *A Book of Americans* (1933).

—JOHN MASON BROWN

DANIEL BOONE

THE OPENING OF THE WILDERNESS

C H A P T E R   I

IMPRISONED IN
A WAGON

AS HE JOLTED ON HIS WAGON SEAT, STOPPING AND starting his horses, then stopping them again, Daniel Boone was not happy. For irksome hours day after day his impatience had grown, while he waited for the engineers far ahead to chop out of the Pennsylvania forest the bumpy road over which he was traveling.

This was a poor, snail's way for a woodsman to move. Daniel's feet longed to touch the ground and to be off at their usual speed, stealing forward in moccasined silence, free of the clatter of wheels. His fingers, hating the reins they held, itched to handle his rifle. His blue eyes were eager to squint and take aim.

This bouncing about in a wagon was not what he had come here for. To be in the rear, choking on the dust of others, was no habit of his. It was an insult to his courage and to his prowess as a hunter. And as a hunter, although less than twenty-one, Daniel was already famous in North Carolina's Yadkin Valley.

The mountains he was crossing interested him. He

had not seen them before. Yet strange as they were, they were also familiar. Since his childhood Daniel had been as much at home in the daytime twilight of primeval forests as most men are in their own houses.

He was never to conquer grammar or spelling, but he had long since conquered the rich and varied language of the woods and come to speak it as a master. "Let the girls do the spelling and Dan will do the shooting," his father, Squire Boone, is rumored to have said. The shooting was what young Daniel was impatient to be doing right now.

The hunting expedition on which he found himself in those June and early July days of 1755 was different from any he had been on before. It was out after bigger

game than all the countless deer, buffalo, and bears he
had shot. It was out after bigger game than he had ever
dreamed of bagging.

Daniel had a lot at stake in this expedition. So did
his relatives and friends in the Yadkin Valley. So did all
the colonists on the Atlantic seaboard. And the French
beyond the mountains and up in Canada. And the Indians of every eastern tribe. So, for that matter, did
Their Royal—but distant—Highnesses, King George II
of England and King Louis XV of France.

The game this time was an enemy stronghold. It was
Fort Duquesne, that fort which the French had built
the year before, where the waters of the Monongahela
and the Allegheny join to form the Ohio, and where
Pittsburgh now stands. They had named it after their
energetic new governor at Quebec.

Fort Duquesne was, of course, more than one of the
several French forts south of Detroit in the great ex-
panses west of the Appalachians. It was a symbol, however shaky, of French power; a proof that France was
determined to fight England for the control of the Mississippi and Ohio Valleys. Its flying the flag of France
especially irritated a certain Colonel George Washington of Virginia. His resentment was natural. He and
his colonial troops had suffered a crushing defeat the
previous summer at nearby Fort Necessity, at the hands
of the French and their Indian allies.

Washington's surrender (the only one of his career)
at Fort Necessity may have soured the Fourth of July

permanently in his memory even when the date had pleasanter associations for him. But the fighting there deserves remembrance. It was the first interchange of shots and casualties in a conflict that was to be fought in Europe, in far-distant Bengal, and on most of the Seven Seas no less than in the forests of North America. In the New World it was known as the French and Indian War; in the Old, as the Seven Years' War.

It was only one war in a series of wars which, though waged under different names and after short periods of peace, was really the same war. This was a long and bloody struggle to determine whether England or France would dominate America. When that question had been settled by English victories, the problem of domination took a new form. In the American Revolution it became a matter of whether the British or the colonists were to control the seaboard and the vast unopened areas beyond the mountains.

Long before—and after—this was decided, another question of control led to fighting of the cruelest and most incessant sort. This was the right of the white men of any nationality to intrude upon and take over lands and the continent on which Indians had lived and hunted, fought and died, for centuries and which they felt were theirs.

This struggle for power, this matter of whose right it was to call the land home, and the surrender at Fort Necessity were among the reasons why Daniel Boone found himself jolting in that wagon toward Fort Duquesne across the Pennsylvania mountains during those early summer days of 1755. On hearing that the British were sending over General Braddock and two redcoated regiments of seven hundred men each, he must have been pleased. He knew the time for fighting it out with the French had come. Even his own people in the Yadkin Valley were living under the threat of Indian scalping parties encouraged and armed by the French.

Accordingly, when the call for volunteers came, Daniel joined up as a militiaman in Major Dobbs' North Carolina company. If he had pictured himself going off to war as a foot soldier or a scout, he was in for a disappointment. It was as a teamster that he was used. And for his teamsters Braddock had, if anything, more contempt than for most of the other colonials serving under him. There being fewer teamsters than he had been guaranteed or needed, they reminded the General of how Benjamin Franklin alone among the officials of the Colonies had lived up to his promises in furnishing horses, wagons, and drivers.

Daniel, on his arrival at Fort Cumberland, was impressed, and perhaps amused, by the British regulars. As a backwoodsman accustomed to wearing deerskin shirt and trousers, he had never dreamed of anything so dazzling as the uniforms these soldiers wore. He had never seen men who carried themselves so straight, who drilled with such precision, or behaved with such arrogance.

It was the short, plump, self-confident figure of Brad-

dock that Daniel gazed at with the greatest awe. Generals were practically unknown in America, and Edward Braddock took being a British general very seriously. He had been one for less than a year when he landed in Virginia. He was a man of sixty who during his forty-five years in the army had seen little action. According to one historian, a considerable time had passed since he had heard a shot more martial than the evening gun at Gibraltar. His temper was fiery, his character invincible, his unwillingness to learn colossal.

The British army was Braddock's religion; the drill manual his bible. He was a parade-ground officer who wanted his troops, even in the wilderness, to look and march as if they were on parade. He knew as little about Indian warfare as Daniel Boone knew about court etiquette. He was shocked by the unsoldierly appearance of the volunteers under his command from New York, Virginia, Maryland, and the Carolinas.

Braddock was no less horrified to learn that these men stooped to fighting the Indians as if they were Indians themselves; in other words, that they broke ranks, deployed through the woods, and hid behind trees or bushes. Yet, stubborn as he was and unacquainted with warfare in the New World, Braddock was a very brave and conscientious man. He was sorely tried by and rightly angered at the Colonies and their failure to furnish him with adequate supplies.

When he left Fort Cumberland, Braddock thought his was a simple task. He knew that three other expeditions were scheduled to move at more or less the same time against the French forts at Niagara, Crown Point on Lake Champlain, and Beausejour in Nova Scotia. The conquest of Fort Duquesne, he believed, would take about four days. Then he would be free to turn north and join the forces at Niagara.

On paper, particularly in London, with no trees to cut down, no road to make, no cannon to haul, no men

and horses to feed, and no mountains to stumble up and
down, it must have seemed easy. Fort Duquesne was
only about one hundred and ten miles away from Fort
Cumberland and, in theory, could be reached in six
comfortably spaced marches. Time was important because Braddock hoped to arrive at the fort before the
French could bring down reinforcements from the north.

Plans on paper have an ugly way of being different
from actions in the field. Braddock's was an overloaded,
slow-moving force which proceeded in the open in close
formation, against an enemy free to hide in the woods.
No wonder one colonist likened it to sending a cow in
pursuit of a hare. Daniel in his wagon unquestionably
had his misgivings during the long hours of waiting and
then inching forward. Why drag howitzers along, he
asked himself, to attack a wooden stockade?

Why wagons and the need to build a twelve-foot road
when pack horses would move more swiftly? Why the
regulars in red coats which were ideal targets? Why
these men all huddled together, inviting danger by not
being spread out? Why so few friendly Indians to serve
as scouts? And why such poor horses and such bad food?
No one could get anywhere at this rate—sometimes
traveling no more than four, three, or two miles a day.

Even Braddock soon came to realize that, instead
of sweeping down on Fort Duquesne, he was crawling
toward it. At Little Meadows he divided his army of
more than 2,000, leaving most of his wagons behind
with the rear group and going ahead himself with a

lightly equipped force of about 1,300. Which of the groups Daniel was with, history does not tell. It seems reasonable to guess, on the basis of what happened, that he was with the forward group.

As the days dragged by until July followed June and July 9th had come, Daniel probably shared the confidence which, from the General down, had begun to spread through Braddock's soldiers. Fort Duquesne was then only twelve miles from Braddock's camp by the shortest route. The forest was clearer, the stretch of land easier. Although there had been some sniping by Indians during the long march, the French had offered no real resistance. The General's plan, after crossing and recrossing the Monongahela, was to make his camp on the night of the 9th a mere seven miles from the fort and, after an easy march, to take it the next day.

Sometime on the 8th of July Daniel had to pull to one side of the road to make way for a wagon that was hurrying to the front. In it was a tall, brown-haired Virginian, aged twenty-three; the same Colonel George Washington who the year before had been compelled to surrender to the French at Fort Necessity. The journey for him in the bouncing wagon was sheer agony. For some weeks he had been a very ill man, the victim of a fever so burning that General Braddock had had to leave him behind at Little Meadows.

The General, however, knowing how special and personal was Washington's interest in this victory over the French, had promised his voluntary aide-de-camp that

he would be present when the fort was taken. On hearing of the General's progress, Washington, though in
pain and still too weak to ride a horse, had hastened
by wagon to rejoin his commander. As it turned out,
by arriving on the 8th he was just in time.

CHAPTER II

HOW *NOT* TO FIGHT INDIANS

THROUGHOUT THE MORNING OF THE 9TH IT MUST HAVE seemed even to Daniel and his fellow wagoners in the rear that everything was going according to schedule. When the second crossing of the Monongahela had been made without resistance, "men hugged themselves with joy" at their good luck. They thought their greatest difficulties were behind them.

Washington was always to remember Braddock's crossing of the river with his redcoats in perfect order as the most thrilling sight of his life. Some of the officers were so confident when they reached Turtle Creek that they expected momentarily to hear a terrific explosion as the French destroyed the fort to prevent its being captured. The noise they heard was not the noise they expected. Instead, it was a deafening burst of scattered shots and an Indian war whoop, paralyzing in its volume. It ripped the air and froze the blood.

Within the wooden stockade of Fort Duquesne the French commander had thought of surrendering. He

was outnumbered. The reinforcements he hoped for had
not arrived; the morale of his men was low. His Indian
allies were frightened. They were dismayed by the ability of the English to move an army over mountains. The
size of that army had been greatly exaggerated by the
Indian scouts who, unseen, had watched it creep forward. Surrender seemed sensible to the commander until
a fearless young Frenchman, Captain Beaujeu, persuaded him to take the chance of facing the English
before they reached the fort.

Beaujeu was permitted to lead an attacking party
which included approximately 250 French and Cana-
dians and some 600 Indians. He would have gone into
action on the 8th of July had not so many of his Indians refused to move until he shamed them by saying
he would go alone. Then they followed him, racing forward toward Turtle Creek until they stumbled upon the
British in country which could not have been more ideal
for the French or fatal for the English.

Along either side, and on higher ground at some distance back from the road being cleared by Braddock's
engineers, were ravines screened by heavy thickets
which the General's scouts had failed to report. They
supplied ready-made trenches and perfect cover. It was
into these ravines that Beaujeu's men darted at his
signal soon after the first shots had been fired at two-
thirty.

Although Beaujeu did not live to reach them himself,
it was from these ravines that the French and Indians

were able to shoot unseen and in comparative safety for three terrible hours during a murderous afternoon. Their targets were hard to miss. They were the British and colonials who, due to General Braddock's brave stupidity, were massed together in the open and trapped in the road that was supposed to lead them to victory.

Daniel Boone may or may not have heard the ghastly war whoop and the thunder of the British volley which answered the enemy's first scattered shots. Certainly he had no way of learning until later what was happening at the front. He could not have known how the

engineers in their surprise and confusion fell back on
the road they were cutting until they ran pell-mell into
the advance party. Or how during the first ten minutes,
when the British vanguard was being raked from three
sides by enemy fire, fifteen out of its eighteen officers
and half of its soldiers had fallen, killed or wounded.

It was not until much later, and then from details
picked up from stray survivors, that Daniel was told the
full, ghastly story. General Braddock, when he heard
the gunfire and the war whoop and saw the confusion,
seemed for some time incapable of doing anything. A
few Englishmen tried to storm the ravines at hideous
cost to themselves. The only sight the British had of the
Indians, unless a painted face became visible for a moment in the trees, was when a warrior would dash forward to scalp a dead foe and then dash back into the
ravines. Braddock was so scandalized, upon seeing the
Virginians break ranks and sensibly spread themselves
in a long line in the woods, that he tried to beat them
back into their earlier formation with the flat of his
sword.

Other details reached Daniel later. The redcoats, in
spite of their bravery, were so packed together that time
after time, on trying to aim at the enemy, they fired
into the backs of their own comrades. Two-thirds of
Braddock's officers and men were slaughtered. The British lost more than 900, the French less than forty.
During the engagement Washington disregarded his ill-
ness and rode for desperate hours. He had two horses

shot out from under him. But fortunately, though bullets pierced his uniform and hat, they left him unscathed.

On this disastrous day Daniel, fretting in his wagon, was also unaware that four of Braddock's mounts were killed before he was struck by a bullet which tore through his right arm and entered his lungs. The wounded General, when the order for retreat had at last been given, was moved to the rear first by wagon, then by litter. Afterwards, when his soldiers refused to carry him further, Braddock was forced, bleeding and in pain, to continue his long journey on horseback. The British General died on the evening of the 13th and was buried, by Washington's order, under the road he had labored to build. After his grave had been filled, the wagons and the troops were commanded to pass over it so that its location could not be found and the General's body mutilated.

All these and a thousand other bits of information about the battle came slowly to Daniel's knowledge. What he knew was only what his eyes saw. This was terrible enough. Where there had been order and silence there was suddenly chaos and noise. It was as if within a narrow gorge a river had turned on itself. What began to rush backward on the slowly advancing soldiers and wagoners was a torrent of human terror, of the maimed, the wounded, the frightened, and the dying. Choked as the road was, rumor ran down it. From man to man the story went that the troops in advance had been wiped out, that the supply wagons were to be attacked next, and that the entire expedition was on the verge of being surrounded and exterminated.

Daniel was seldom to know fear, but this time panic seized him. He found himself in a stampede of horses and men. Jumping from his wagon, he cut one of his horses loose, leaped on its back, and headed for home.

Daniel was not the only wagoner to run away. Another was John Finley. He was one of several men in Braddock's army who had already hunted in the beckoning forests and rich lands south of the Ohio. Night after night over the campfire during the slow march toward Fort Duquesne, Finley had told Daniel about the great forests, the sunny clearings, and the limitless buffalo and game to be found in this country which the Indians called "Kentucky." As he described its beauties and wonders, he compared it to a second Garden of Eden. And Daniel had listened with a quickened heart.

Thirteen years were to slip by before Daniel saw Finley again. Then it was by chance when Finley rode up with his peddler's pack to the Boones' cabin in the Yadkin Valley. During all that time Daniel had not forgotten Finley's words. They had haunted him like a dream. He had wanted to remember them even as he must have tried to forget the nightmare of Braddock's defeat.

Certainly, Daniel did not come out of his first battle a hero. But he had learned a lot. Among other things he had learned how *not* to fight Indians. Although he may

He leaped on the horse's back, and headed for home

have arrived at Fort Cumberland a youth, he returned to the Yadkin an adult. His boyhood, however, was an essential preparation for what he was to do in the years to come when he would make history—instead of run away from it.

C H A P T E R   I I I

MORE ELBOWROOM

DANIEL CAME FROM A FAMILY THAT WAS ALWAYS ON the move. Some people like the security of staying in places they know and where they are known. Some people, even if they dislike the noise, the crowds, the unfresh air, and the grassless streets of cities, like the comfort which comes from having neighbors. Some people are happy to remain on the settled side of the mountain.

Not the Boones. Not Grandfather George nor Daniel's father, whose odd first name was Squire. Certainly not Daniel, nor most of his brothers and sons, nor his grandsons, one of whom is said to have been Kit Carson, the famous hunter and scout. The Boones wanted land where deer and buffalo were numerous and men and cabins scarce.

They wanted to be on the fringe of civilization, not in its midst. They wanted the freedom of a wilderness really wild, and were constantly selling the land they owned and pushing on if the wilderness showed signs of being tamed. When Daniel, as an old man, was asked why he was leaving a settlement once again for the frontier, his answer was, "Too crowded. I want more elbowroom!"

The Boones were always wanting more elbowroom. When they had explored, hunted, or settled a new territory, other families were forever following them there until this elbowroom was lost. Then the Boones would head westward again.

There was Daniel's grandfather, for example. He was a Quaker and a weaver who, though he knew some troubles in England because of his religion, lived contentedly enough in Devon. At least he did until he began to hear stories about Pennsylvania, the great young Quaker colony in the New World. These reports stirred his imagination, just as more than forty years later, by the campfires on the road to Fort Duquesne, John Finley's tales about Kentucky captured Daniel's mind. George Boone was tempted to leave England.

Like all the Boones, including Daniel, George was a cautious man, though brave. Before making up his mind, he wanted to learn more about the land to which he was thinking of taking his family. He solved the problem of how to do this in his own way. In 1712 he sent a daughter Sarah and two of his sons, George and Squire, ahead to see if they approved of what Pennsylvania offered. Apparently they did, because four years later the older George and his family made the final break.

They arrived in Philadelphia on October 10, 1717, after nearly eight weeks at sea. Everyone except town-

lovers wanted land in those days. Land was the fever of the times. It represented freedom no less than food. Men sweated to chop down the forest so that they could farm and be their own masters. The Boones farmed only as much as they had to. They were more interested in the animals which roamed in the woods than in the crops which grew in the soil.

For a year they lived at Abingdon near Philadelphia. Then they moved to Oley in Berks County (not far from Reading). There Daniel was born in 1734 and spent his boyhood. The region, filled at first with game, began little by little to be occupied by settlers. This was more than Squire Boone, Daniel's father, could stand.

By 1750 he was suffering from the old Boone complaint, lack of elbowroom. He sold his land and pushed on to find a new home where he would not be crowded. He had no destination; he had only a desire to move on. Accordingly, he and his family started on their way, the women and children in wagons, the boys and men on horseback, driving their cattle before them.

It was not an easy journey. There were streams to ford, camps to pitch, Indians to fear, and watches to stand. They headed southwest across Pennsylvania, then down the Cumberland Valley, and next the Shenandoah in Virginia, until in North Carolina they reached the Yadkin. In this valley, five hundred long, hard miles from their starting point, they settled. They had found country primitive enough to satisfy them and alive with game. To the west, forming a wall mighty and mysterious, were the mountains which no white man had yet dared to cross.

Daniel was about eighteen when he reached the Yadkin. The land was a hunter's paradise. It abounded in bears and deer; in beavers, otters, and muskrats; in wildcats, panthers, and wolves; in turkeys and many other wild fowl. If these soon became fewer, it was because of Daniel. Back in Berks County he had already mastered both the rifle and the woods. No one knows whether he ever went to school indoors, but he never stopped going to school out-of-doors.

His spelling, which someone had taught him, was never so certain as his shooting, which he had taught himself. Even before he was given his first gun he was an excellent marksman. The weapon he made for himself as a boy was a stick with a cluster of roots at one end. His aim with this was so accurate that neither birds nor small game were safe from him.

A woodsman, a real woodsman of Daniel's kind, is more than a man who is happiest in the woods and has learned every lesson they have to teach him. A true woodsman has no fear of the sounds heard in the woods by night or the wild animals stumbled upon by day.

Even the thought of being absolutely alone in them does not frighten him. If he really knows the woods, the woodsman knows that their very silence will talk to him.

Daniel had learned to be a woodsman as a boy. When he was ten, his father had bought twenty-five acres for grazing purposes a few miles away from their Pennsylvania home. Until he was sixteen Daniel and his mother, Sarah, went each summer to these lonely acres to fatten the family's cattle on better pastures. The two of them lived in a rough log cabin there, while Squire Boone stayed at home, dividing his time between weaving and blacksmithing.

Daniel's job was to drive the cows out in the morning and round them up at night. As they grazed, Daniel hunted. He hunted at first with the wooden weapon he had made for himself, and later with the long rifle his father had given him. He did not kill merely for the fun of it. He killed in order to live. The deer he brought in were needed for food and clothing, and the skins sold for good prices in Philadelphia.

Daniel was as familiar with Indians as he was with other dwellers in the forest. He had known them since he was a baby in Berks County. Although in the Quaker colony there had been threats of trouble, Pennsylvania had been spared the sudden scalping parties and terrible massacres all too common elsewhere along the frontier. The Quakers had lived up to their name of "Friends." They had treated the Indians far better than most other white settlers. This is why the Indians Daniel saw as a child were peaceful.

The Indians he had known in Berks County were Delawares. They had visited his grandfather's farm either as guests or as welcome braves who had become Quakers and preached the night through at meetings in the barns at Oley. Daniel had observed them carefully. He noted how quietly they moved through the woods and the animal instinct they showed in hiding behind a tree or becoming a part of nature. He knew more than their customs. He understood their thoughts. There are those who have said that even as a youth he could "think Indian," a fact which was to save his life on many occasions in the dangerous years that lay ahead.

Later on, when his family had settled in the Yadkin Valley, establishing their farm, their looms, and a forge, Daniel had only one unhappy encounter with a red man. In contest after contest he was foolish enough to out-shoot a brave who finally became so outraged by these defeats that he announced he was going to kill Daniel. The brave disappeared when he heard that Daniel's father, forgetting the peaceful ways of the Quakers, had gone out, hatchet in hand, to get the man who was threatening his son.

This experience was not wasted on Daniel. It taught him how to keep Indians friendly by pretending he could not shoot as well as they could. This knowledge was to prove valuable.

CHAPTER IV

HISTORY
COMES KNOCKING

WHEN HE SERVED AS A WAGONER WITH GENERAL BRAD-
dock's ill-fated army, Daniel had his first encounter
with hostile Indians and warfare. The youth who volunteered for that disastrous campaign had returned to the
Yadkin a man. A man, according to him, needed three
things to be happy—"a good gun, a good horse, and a
good wife." Daniel already had a gun and a horse (both
good). Within about a year he had a wife (also good).

She was a girl of seventeen with jet black hair and
eyes, named Rebecca Bryan. Her father, Joseph Bryan,
was a neighbor whose brother had married one of Daniel's sisters. The Bryans and the Boones were families
who already had a lot in common and were to have
more. They, too, were people who liked plenty of elbowroom. They, too, had made the long trek from Pennsylvania, and with the Boones were to continue moving
westward.

The life Rebecca faced as Daniel's wife was not easy.
It was as hard and rough as the frontier itself. Daniel's

Within about a year he had a wife

mother had endured the same kind of life but without the dangers Rebecca faced when the Indians, who had been friendly, went on the warpath. Rebecca was to know few comforts, no luxuries, and many dangers in the long years ahead. She was not the only woman of her kind. If there had not been hundreds of others as stout-hearted as their husbands, the West would have remained unsettled.

The log cabins these pioneer women called home were crude structures. They were dark and primitive; not so much houses as shelters. Wives had little time to rest in them. They had food to cook, clothing to make, bullets and candles to mold, butter to churn, large families to raise, and illnesses to nurse.

In the bloody times of war they never knew when they would hear sudden war whoops at their doors, see tomahawks crush the skulls of their children, or feel the scalping knife slash their own heads. They were trained and ready to reach for rifles themselves. Many of them lived, as Rebecca did, not knowing sometimes for a year or two whether their husbands and sons, away hunting or fighting, were free men or prisoners, dead or alive.

Major Dobbs' North Carolina militiamen, who had served in Pennsylvania with Braddock, had joined up in the hope of keeping the French and Indian War away from their own homes. Within two years of Daniel's and Rebecca's marriage, however, the Yadkin Valley suffered the terrors of Indian attack. Little by little, the

French were losing their control of the vast territory
to the west. The English were taking over and would remain all-powerful until this region, with its wavering
Indian allies, was once again fought for during the
Revolution.

Fort Duquesne had been captured by the British in
1758 and renamed Fort Pitt after the elder William
Pitt, Britain's great Prime Minister. Daniel may or may
not have jostled fretfully as a wagoner on this expedition. As an old man he did mention killing his first Indian at the "Juniata Bridge," which was on the route
to Fort Duquesne.

In any case, what Braddock's men had dreamed of
three years before had happened at last. Rather than
have the fort fall into English hands, the French had
blown it up. There was only the strategic site to take,
that and the bodies of some British and American prisoners burned so that their scalped heads resembled
scorched pumpkins.

The retreating French tried to make the best of their
defeat. They sent agents far and wide to persuade the
Indians who had buried the tomahawk to dig it up and
go on the warpath.

Among the once peaceful Indians that responded
were the Cherokees. This southern tribe, as powerful as
it was fierce, was soon creeping through the woods
which led to North Carolina's western frontier. They
had their excellent reasons for fighting. Several Cherokee braves had been killed without warning by some

English colonists who had no cause for these murders
except their fear and hatred of Indians.

In the ugly struggle which followed, the Boones left
their farm and cabin in order to save their children.
Daniel and Rebecca with their two infant sons found

safety in Culpeper County, Virginia. They stayed in
Virginia for two years. The Cherokees had by then been
defeated, their villages wiped out, their crops ruined,
and their people driven to lands which could not feed
them. They made peace, and with its coming Daniel
and Rebecca returned to the Yadkin and purchased a
large tract there.

The land Daniel owned was never the land he wanted to be on for long. The next few years found him wandering constantly. How far he traveled the forests themselves tell. Daniel had a strange fondness for keeping a brief diary on beech trees. His spelling changed with the places and the years. On one trip to Tennessee he carved a famous inscription reading, "D Boon cilled A BAR on this tree year 1760." Thirteen years later, on another tree in Tennessee, he was to write, "D Boon killa bar on this tree 1773." Once he recorded his finding of a clear spring by writing on a beech, "Come on boys here's good water."

He roamed as far south as Florida, where he would have starved to death if the Seminole Indians had not shared their food with him. He bought a house and property in Pensacola, hoping Rebecca and their growing family would join him. But on his return to the Yadkin Rebecca spoke up for once and said, "No." She could not imagine Daniel in a country without the game he was accustomed to shooting.

Thereafter he dreamed more and more of the land on the other side of the mountains. In addition to the several journeys he made to Tennessee, he strayed into eastern Kentucky with some friends, shooting his first buffalo and spending a winter there. His only disappointment was that the country through which he traveled was not the open country John Finley had described on the way to Fort Duquesne. Daniel had not found the secret door to the great mountain wall which separated him from the new and summoning lands beyond.

Then one fall day a peddler chanced to ride up to the Boone cabin in the Yadkin. Of all people, he turned out to be John Finley. He and history had come to Daniel's door at the same time.

CHAPTER V

THE SECRET DOOR

IF JOHN FINLEY HAD NOT STOPPED AT THE BOONES' cabin, Daniel might never have been known, except to his neighbors as a hunter in the Yadkin Valley. Men's lives are changed in odd ways without their realizing it. A boat missed, a talk with a stranger, a thoughtless choice at the crossroads to turn right instead of left, or a knock on a door, and not only can a man's living be altered but history can be given a new course. Both of these things happened when John Finley rode up to the home of the Boones.

Not having seen each other for nearly fourteen years, Daniel and Finley had a lot to talk about. Since Finley spent the winter with the Boones, they had plenty of time to get their talking done. Finley did most of the talking. He was still talking Kentucky, and with the same enthusiasm. He had visited Kentucky again the year before, traveling down the Ohio by canoe and trading with the Indians. On the way back he had faced the difficulty of paddling upstream against a strong current.

From the Indians Finley had learned that the secret door Daniel had been looking for in the mountains really did exist. He had also heard that leading to this door was a trail used by red hunters and war parties.

This trail, the "Warriors' Path," may even have been followed in years past by a few white men. Travel on it was apparently very hard. Yet, if woodsmen who knew the forest could come upon this trail, it would mean much. The Ohio's dangerous eddies, snags, and fickle currents could be avoided. An overland route would be available. The new lands to the west, so long guarded by the frowning mountains, could at last be reached.

And what tempting lands they were! As John Finley

described them night after night, they were a hunters' dream. Innumerable birds. So many wild turkeys in the woods that they seemed to belong to a single endless flock. Passenger pigeons migrating in such numbers that often they blotted out the sun for three days at a time and darkened the sky like black clouds. There were buffalo, too; buffalo so plentiful that a man had to be agile to avoid being trampled to death when a herd stampeded.

Moreover, the landscape was beautiful and ever-changing. There were mountains and magnificent forests. There were canebrakes and lovely rivers cutting their way deep through limestone cliffs. There were inviting stretches of gently rolling country. There were trees, mighty and luxuriant. The soil was bursting with fertility, the grass a sea of blue. There were carpets of clover and sweet-scented wildflowers splashing the summer's greenness with bright colors.

Yes, of course, there were Indians, and of many tribes. John Finley had to admit this. But, as he made clear, even the Indians felt differently about Kentucky. They did not live there. They hunted there. To the Indians Kentucky was a magical land left unsettled. It was a wilderness kept free for hunting or fighting.

Each spring braves from such of the Algonquin tribes to the north as the Wyandots, the Mingos, and the Shawnees would head for the rich land south of the Ohio River. Each spring braves from such an Appalachian tribe to the south as the Cherokees would push northward from Tennessee to the same great meadows. Although generally they were after game, sometimes hostile tribes would meet and fight so fiercely that the region was known as "the Dark and Bloody Ground."

The thought of Indians did not frighten Daniel or his friends as they listened to John Finley, and he suggested their going with him to Kentucky in the spring. They already knew a lot about Indians. Danger had always been as much a part of their lives as breathing. Anyway, Finley had had no trouble in Kentucky the year before. What mattered was not the red men beyond the mountains but the new country. Finley spoke about it in such tempting terms that Daniel must have thought the winter months would never end.

He was impatient to get started. His brother-in-law, John Stuart, was no less anxious and so were three other Yadkin neighbors. Daniel's brother, Squire, would have gone with them, had it not been decided that he should stay at home until he had harvested his own and Daniel's crops. The plan was that he would then meet them in Kentucky with fresh horses and supplies, including ammunition.

On the first day of May, 1769, the six men set off. Each was riding a horse and leading a second horse loaded with a pack saddle. They took with them salt, camp kettles, traps, a little food, and blankets or bearskins. All of them had their long rifles swung across their shoulders. At their belts they carried tomahawks, hunting knives,

Looking down from a high ridge . . . Daniel was filled with delight

powder horns, and bullet pouches. They wore deerskin shirts, trousers, and moccasins.

Regardless of what the other five men may have had on their heads, one thing seems certain. Daniel Boone was *not* wearing a coonskin cap. As a rule, frontiersmen liked coonskin caps. But not Daniel. Contrary to all legends and most hopes, historians agree he had no use for them. He wore a tall black hat. How he kept it on his head when the winds blew or he swam rivers, and what its color was if and when he still had it on when he came home, is not explained. Histories merely state that he did not wear a coonskin cap.

The party of six moved forward slowly across the Blue Ridge Mountains through dense forests, leaving the last white settlement behind them and edging into the unknown. Their luck was with them when it came to locating the door through the mountains which they hoped to find. In the speckled shadows of the woods they stumbled upon the kind of lightly marked trail known as a hunter's "trace."

This led them to the Cumberland Gap, that natural gateway where Virginia, Tennessee, and Kentucky touch. Earlier explorers, such as Dr. Thomas Walker, had already passed through it. Though these men had come back with exciting stories, their explorations had not resulted in the opening of the new country to the west. The moment for that had not then come. Now it was at hand.

At the Gap, Daniel and his companions were again

fortunate. They came across the Warriors' Path about which John Finley had heard and it led them through the mountains and, at last, into Kentucky. Looking down from a high ridge on the rich and gentle lands spread out below him, Daniel was filled with delight. This Kentucky was all that he had imagined and everything Finley had said it would be. He little dreamed what it would mean to him and he to it, or of the adventures he would have there.

CHAPTER VI

THE STING
OF WASPS

PUSHING ON, DANIEL AND HIS PARTY ESTABLISHED A
main base on Station Camp Creek. They then set about
their serious business, which was hunting. Their hope
was to return to the Yadkin with enough valuable
pelts to pay for their expedition and make a comfortable profit.

As the summer stretched into fall and fall into winter,
everything seemed to be in their favor. Daniel was
later to say this was the happiest period in his life. He
was doing what he liked best under ideal conditions.
Neither he nor the men with him had ever seen so much
game. Having come across no signs of Indians, they began to think they had the woods to themselves.

Nonetheless they took precautions. They would go
out from their main camp in pairs, hunting by day and
spending their nights at smaller camps which were no
more than shelters. At these they would smoke such
meat as they wished to preserve, and scrape and cure
the skins they had collected. After they had gathered as

much as they could carry, they would return to Station Camp Creek. Once there, to protect the skins from bears, wolves, and weather, they would cover them with bark and stack them on racks raised high above the ground.

The hunting continued to be excellent when the rich green woods began to flame with color, and even afterwards, when many of the trees were bare. As the months passed, the bales of skins grew and grew in number. Since these piles represented money, Daniel and his companions were happy as they watched them grow.

With the coming of winter, the white hunters learned they had made a fatal mistake. They had invited trouble by building their main camp and their shelters too near the Warriors' Path over which any Indians passing through Kentucky were certain to travel.

Daniel and John Stuart were the first to discover the cost of this error. Late in the afternoon of December 22, 1769, when they were on a little hill near the Kentucky River, a band of Shawnee horsemen, appearing from nowhere, surrounded them and took them prisoner. The Indians did them no physical harm. Brandishing their tomahawks as a reminder of what they could do, they commanded Stuart and Daniel to lead them first to the outlying shelters and next to the main camp.

John Finley and the three other white men had warning of the Indians' approach. Daniel was, therefore, appalled to discover they had saved themselves by taking to the woods without doing anything to save either their horses or their large store of skins. He and Stuart,

burning with anger, were forced in their helplessness to
appear friendly. They had to stand by while the Indians
stole everything, including the precious furs it had taken
seven months to collect.

Freed within a few days, Daniel and Stuart were told
to get out of Kentucky. They were supplied with guns

and enough ammunition to provide themselves with
food on the way back.

"Now, brothers," said Captain Will, the Shawnee
chief who spoke some English, "go home and stay there.
Don't come here any more, for this is the Indians' hunting ground and all the animals, skins, and furs are ours.
If you are so foolish as to come here again, you may be
sure the wasps and yellow jackets will sting you
severely."

This was the Indians' warning. When the chief had
finished speaking, the two white men shook hands with
the Shawnees and left them. Rather, they pretended to
leave them, for Daniel and John Stuart were not the
kind to give up easily.

Keeping well under cover, they shadowed the red
men. Then one night, when the Shawnees were sleeping,
they managed to recapture four or five of their horses.
Galloping away, they covered so many miles that they
thought they were safe. At sunrise, however, when they
were resting, they were horrified to find the red men had
overtaken them. They were again surrounded and made
prisoners.

Considering that Stuart and Daniel had already been
given one warning, the threatened sting of the Shawnee
"wasps and yellow jackets" was unusually mild. The
warriors had their fun with Daniel. Once while they
shouted, "Steal horse, ha?" and laughed, they made
him trot with a bell tied around his neck like one of the
horses he had recaptured. But they did not make their

captives run the gauntlet. Better still, they left their scalps untouched.

The Indians' plan was to carry the two men north with them to Ohio. The only trouble with this plan was that it did not take Daniel into account. He had his own ideas. He had studied the Indian character since he was a boy, and when it came to tricks he could be as tricky as any brave.

For seven days Daniel acted as if he were glad to be with his Shawnee "friends" and urged Stuart to do the same. Daniel was to play this game often in the future, and always with success. By means of it he won the confidence of his captors and they grew careless in guarding him.

On the seventh night, when the party had nearly reached the Ohio River and a long imprisonment in the lands to the north seemed certain, Daniel waited until everyone was asleep. Then he crept over to Stuart, woke him up, and the two men moved noiselessly about the campfire on their moccasins. After they had gathered the rifles, bullets, and powder they needed, they made a dash in the darkness for the nearby canebrake—and liberty.

Although Daniel and Stuart had hoped to rejoin their friends at Station Camp, they found it deserted and pushed on towards the settlements, heavy of heart but swift of foot. They had gone only a short way when they came across John Finley and his three companions.

Finley and his companions, thinking that Daniel and Stuart must have been killed, were already on their way home. They had had more than their fill of Kentucky's hardships and dangers. And, regardless of what Daniel said, home they went, disappearing into the woods and from history, too.

CHAPTER VII

ALONE IN KENTUCKY

DANIEL AND STUART MIGHT HAVE GONE WITH FINLEY and the others had not two men, who from a distance looked very much like Indians, suddenly come towards them. Daniel had his rifle aimed and was ready to shoot when, to his surprise and joy, he discovered that one of these men was his brother Squire.

In spite of distance, perils, the lack of communications, and the swallowing immensity of the wilderness, Squire had come to join Daniel just as he had promised. He was bringing fresh supplies, horses, and ammunition. Moreover, he had news about Rebecca and the children for which Daniel hungered. With him was a friend, Alexander Neeley, whose presence meant another "gun."

The dark picture brightened for Daniel. Where a few minutes before everything had seemed hopeless, it now looked as if the expedition of the Boones, instead of being a sorry failure, had a chance to prove successful after all.

The four men set up a new camp farther away from

48

the Warriors' Path and started hunting and trapping.
Squire and Neeley went out as one pair, Daniel and
Stuart as another. Although once they had to shoot off
a party of Indians who interrupted a nighttime reading
of *Gulliver's Travels* by the campfire, they ran into no
serious trouble until late January or early February,
1770.

It was then that John Stuart failed to come back to a
place where he and Daniel had agreed to meet. Daniel,
who had a brother's fondness for Stuart, started looking for him after a few days of anxious waiting. He came
across the remains of a fire which Stuart had probably
built. Of Stuart himself he found no trace until five
years later, in a hollow sycamore tree, he chanced upon
a skeleton beside which was a powder horn bearing
Stuart's initials. No one ever learned the cause of Stuart's death. His disappearance, however, unnerved
Neeley who, frankly admitting his dislike of a country
in which it was so easy for a man to vanish or be murdered, hurried back to Carolina.

Although the Boones must have been discouraged,
they were undaunted. They built a hut and kept on with
their trapping until the spring had come. Then, their
ammunition being low, they reached a difficult decision.

One of them would have to go back to the Yadkin to
sell their large stock of furs, skins, and jerked meat, and
then return with more supplies. The other, not to waste
precious time, would have to stay in Kentucky. His
tasks would be many and important. He would have to

master the secrets of the shadow-filled forests. He would
have to explore the green valleys or sheltering canebrakes. He would have to follow the paths beaten down
by the hoofs of buffalo and animals of all kinds, which
led to the many salt licks where the hunting was certain
to be fine.

It was Squire who went home, and Daniel who remained in Kentucky—alone. He wanted to go with
Squire. He ached to see Rebecca and the children. A full
year had passed since that May day when he had left
his family. Daniel, however, felt he owed too much
money to his neighbors in the Yadkin Valley to face
them or Rebecca until he could come to them, able to
pay his debts and justify their faith in him.

He stayed on—without bread, salt or sugar, without
a horse or even a dog. His one and only companion was
"Tick-Licker," the long rifle he liked best; and, since
Daniel had little ammunition, he had to do all he could
to keep "Tick-Licker" from talking too much.

Luckily Squire Boone reached the Yadkin without
mishap, sold their furs, and paid their debts. Three
months later, at the end of July, he rejoined Daniel,
bringing fresh supplies. As winter approached, Squire
again left for Carolina, making another successful trip
and returning two months later with new supplies.

Few men could have been better equipped by tem-
perament or training than Daniel to spend first three,
then two, months alone in the wilderness. Yet these five

months of solitude during his second year away from home must often have been a trial even to Daniel.

To be sure, he had his woodsman's pleasures. He wandered far, his ever-alert eyes delighting in what they saw. He was amazed at the richness of the vegetation and admired the trees—the sycamores, the honey locusts, the tulip trees, and the black mulberries—among which he broke his way. He was fascinated by the mineral springs—Big Lick, Big Bone Lick, and the Blue Licks— and the fossilized bones of huge mastodons which they held captive in their soft soil. He was thrilled, too, by the sight of thousands of buffalo licking the earth at these springs, and then dashing away clumsily and dangerously at his approach.

A land bulging with deer, elk, bears, and wild turkeys was a land he liked. He had the fun of naming unnamed places and streams. He had the satisfaction of seeing, as John Finley had assured him he would, the ruins of a French stockade at the Falls of the Ohio where Louis-ville now is. He had the pleasure of journeying up and down the Kentucky River where, at Big Lick, Boones-borough would one day be built.

Yet, except for the silent language his senses spoke to him incessantly, the only talk Daniel heard was the sudden noises of the forest which could be surprising by day and alarming by night. He was a man always in danger, hence always on guard, with no one to replace him as a sentinel.

If, free as he was, Daniel was condemned to living a fugitive's life, it was because he never knew at what turn or behind which bushes or clumps of trees Indians might be crouched, with their guns pointed or their tomahawks raised. He kept on the move, changing his camps, hiding his tracks, and seeking refuge in thickets, canebrakes, and caves. For food Daniel probably depended a great deal on berries, since a fire for cooking or the crack of his rifle would have let warriors know where he was.

Unlike many frontiersmen, Daniel was never a killer of Indians for the sport of killing them. When he shot a red man it was because a red man might shoot him. Once during his lonely days and nights in Kentucky, he did let "Tick-Licker" do some talking. He saw an Indian fishing from a tree trunk. As the Indian might have seen him, Daniel permitted "Tick-Licker" to speak up. Years later Daniel used to describe what happened by saying, with a solemn face, "While I was looking at the fellow he tumbled into the river, and I saw him no more." Daniel could take no chances.

Once, too, wandering by a creek on a cliff sixty feet high, he discovered to his horror that a band of braves was closing in on him from three sides. His only hope of escape was to jump. So jump he did, landing on the crest of a sugar maple he had noticed below him. He slipped down the tree, swiftly swam the stream, and disappeared into the underbrush on the far bank to the accompaniment of a good many startled and disap-

pointed "Ughs" from the Indians who gazed down on
him from the cliff.

How much Daniel enjoyed the kind of life he lived
in Kentucky can be guessed by the story a group of
forty Virginians, known as "the Long Hunters," had to

tell of him. These men, expert woodsmen all, had been
out in the wilderness for more than a year on a highly
successful hunting expedition. Not ready as yet to return to the settlements, they were nonetheless heading
homeward. They had reached the Green River when

one late afternoon they heard a noise such as the most
experienced of them had never heard.

As they paused, frozen with alarm, their leader
snaked his way from tree to tree toward the source of
the sound. He was expecting to find either a strange
animal or an Indian giving a signal which would lead

them into a trap. He could not believe his eyes when, instead of coming on a brave or an unknown beast, he found "a man bare-headed, stretched flat upon his back on a deerskin spread on the ground, singing merrily at the top of his voice!" It was Daniel, for once incautious and perhaps not much of a singer, but definitely very happy.

Daniel was happier still when Squire, a little later than he said he would be, rejoined him and the two brothers had some months of profitable hunting with the "Long Hunters." He was no less happy when he and Squire left these hunters in March and at last turned their horses toward the Yadkin.

Although the Boones had borrowed heavily for this final expedition, they were not worried. They were carrying home a staggering load of furs. When their debts were paid, they would still have a comfortable amount of money for their families. Squire's rugged efforts, and Daniel's two years of absence and his five months of solitude, had not been in vain.

In high spirits, they came closer and closer to the Yadkin, indeed so close that they reached Powell's Valley, near the Cumberland Gap, on the very fringe of the settlements. But just when they thought they were safe, a war party of northern Indians swooped down on them, robbing them of all they had struggled so hard and valiantly to collect.

Daniel's homecoming was a sad one. He was experiencing cruelly that bad luck with pelts, land, money, and possessions which was to plague him throughout his long life. Even so, he had seen Kentucky, and had come to know it as few men did. He counted this knowledge his good fortune, not realizing it was to be Kentucky's, too.

CHAPTER VIII

THE FIRE
IS LIGHTED

DANIEL SPENT THE NEXT TWO AND A HALF YEARS MAIN-
ly with his family. As usual, during the autumn and
winter he roamed far and wide, hunting either alone or
with friends. He even visited Kentucky again, and in
the land beyond the mountains he once more enjoyed
the fullness of life. This joy was in his heart when he
returned to Rebecca and the children, and because of it
he had reached a new decision.

He had come to realize that, though his home was in
the Yadkin Valley, he no longer felt at home there. He
was not happy now in the settlements. The smoke from
too many chimneys spoiled the air for him; the sight of
too many people ruined the view. He needed money
and, as a hunter, he found money hard to come by in a
region where game was so scarce that hunting had
ceased to be either profitable or pleasant.

Daniel was disturbed, too, by what had been happening in North Carolina. The trouble, which had begun
before he left for his two lonely years in Kentucky,

reached a bloody climax about the time he came back
empty-handed. The taxes levied by a ruthless royal
governor were unbearably high and dishonestly collected.

Some angry colonists, known as the "Regulators,"
protested by taking the law into their own hands. The
mob violence to which they resorted was not stopped
until they had been routed in battle by the militia and
seven of their leaders executed. In the back country the
memory of the battle lasted along with the bitter feelings which had provoked it.

Men and women who are discontented and think
themselves badly treated listen to words the happy do
not hear. The widespread dissatisfaction and unrest of
Daniel's friends and neighbors made it the easier for
him to persuade them that the time had come to escape
from such injustices and find freedom in the wilderness.

To be a hunter wandering in a strange land is one
thing; to move and build there as a settler and call it
home quite another. Daniel was ready to make this
change. He decided to sell his farm and cabin, to uproot
himself and his family, and with them to leave the Yadkin for a new life in the new country.

Rebecca was willing to go with him. So, after Daniel
had talked to them, were five families whose farms were
close to his. And so were Daniel's old friends and Rebecca's relatives, the Bryans. The Bryans, however, like
the large party of men they recruited from Powell's Val-

ley and the Valley of Virginia, did not want to take their wives and children until a settlement had been built.

The risks were serious; the only certainties danger and discomfort. The Indians had already told Daniel what all white intruders might expect. There was no doubt about it. The "wasps and yellow jackets" would sting severely this time. If the red men resented whites who came to hunt, they could be counted on to show no mercy to whites who came to stay.

Even the law was against Boone and his expedition. As far back as 1763 King George III had issued a proclamation forbidding his "loving subjects" to settle beyond the mountains. Apparently His Majesty's government was sincere in its wish to keep the Indians peaceful, and hence protect its subjects on the border. Either this, or it had its own plans for developing the fur trade and wanted to keep taxable colonists within reach.

Daniel and his party, however, were determined to set out. Living in the back country, they felt safely beyond the control of London and too far from the colonial governor to be stopped by orders which were almost impossible to enforce. Furthermore, they comforted themselves by believing that certain hazy treaties, signed by the Iroquois in the north and the Cherokees in the south, had given them the right to settle in Kentucky.

Full of confidence, Daniel and his group left the Yadkin on September 25, 1773. They were slowed down by pack horses carrying their household goods and the cattle they drove before them. When they had crossed several mountain ranges, they camped in Powell's Valley where, as agreed, they were to be joined by the parties raised by the Bryans and Captain William Russell.

While they were waiting, Daniel discovered that, in spite of careful planning, more flour and farming tools were needed. The person he sent back to Russell's farm to collect these was his sixteen-year-old son James. Daniel was very close to James, who shared his father's love of the woods and had been taken by him on hunting expeditions since he was eight. Inasmuch as they were still near the settlements, James' present assignment seemed safe. And safe it would have been, had not James and Russell's son, with two slaves and two white helpers, lost their way on the return trip.

They did not know they were only three miles from Daniel's party, and decided to make camp as darkness came on, thinking that next day they could find the trail they had missed. But for all of them, except one white man and a slave who escaped, there was to be no next day. Before dawn, while still sleeping, they were attacked by Indians and murdered after a long torture. During this agony James, his hips pierced by a bullet, his body covered with gashes, his fingernails ripped out, and his hands slashed from fighting off knives, was heard to scream, begging his tormentors to kill him quickly.

James' death was so much stone in Daniel's and Rebecca's hearts, and reports of the massacre's brutality proved disastrous to the expedition the Boones were heading. Most of its members, in spite of Daniel's pleas, were unwilling to go on. Appalled by what had happened and afraid of what might happen, the little band turned back, its once brave hopes shattered. Those who still had homes to go to returned to them.

Daniel, having no home, was determined to stay as near as he could to Kentucky. He moved his family for the winter into a friend's abandoned cabin on the Clinch River in Tennessee. How dear to his thoughts James and Kentucky continued to be, Daniel showed in the spring by making a lonely journey to James' grave.

News of the Indians' massacre of James and his party soon reached the settlements, filling them with anger and demands for revenge. The atmosphere on both sides

of the mountains was tense. White men were found killed in their corn fields without warning, and so were young braves. The Indians betrayed their mood by accepting only rifles, ammunition, knives, and hatchets in payment for their furs. The colonists showed their feeling by joining the militia and backing up Lord Dunmore, the unpopular and dictatorial governor of Virginia, when he talked openly of war.

The fire was laid, waiting to be lighted. A torch which set it blazing was the treacherous murder of several Indians by three cruel and stupid traders. The Indians who were slain had thought themselves safe. They were being entertained as friends by the three frontiersmen. Their party included the sister, the brother, and another relative of the powerful Mingo leader, Chief Logan, who until this time was famous as a champion of peace.

Chief Logan learned of the slaughter of his family at the very moment he was speaking eloquently to a council of Mingos, trying as usual to persuade them not to fight their white brothers. His feelings changed at once. An understandable hatred fired his heart.

He dug up the war hatchet he had just buried and, lifting it above his head, took a solemn oath that nothing and no one could stop him until he had killed ten white people for every member of his family murdered. A chief who had fought for peace was now as eager as the most bloodthirsty of the Mingo braves to fight a war.

CHAPTER IX

WAR ON THE FRONTIER

THE MINGOS WERE NOT THE ONLY RED MEN ANXIOUS for the tests of battle. The Cherokees and Shawnees were also carrying war pipes from village to village, daubing their faces and bodies with paint, droning their fierce chants, dancing their wild dances, and preparing for a bitter fight.

The colonists, no less aroused, were making their own preparations. Every man and boy capable of carrying a gun was called into the militia. Forts were built in the frontier valleys. Scouts were sent out to locate Indian forces and report on their activities. Lord Dunmore was determined not to wait to be attacked but to carry the fight into the Indians' own country.

Before making the first move, he hoped to reach and recall several parties of surveyors he had sent into the wilderness in spite of King George's proclamation. Two of these parties—one headed by James Harrod, the other by Thomas Bullitt—had entered Kentucky by the Ohio River, now blockaded by the Shawnees. Another group led by George Washington's agent, John Floyd, had come in by the Kanawha. All were in the greatest danger, if indeed they were still alive. They were brave men, too valuable to lose, who needed a brave man to save them.

Colonel William Preston as commandant of the southwest militia ordered Captain William Russell to send "two faithful woodsmen" into Kentucky to warn these surveyors. The first person Russell thought of was his old friend Daniel Boone. To go with him, he selected Michael Stoner, another master woodsman.

The distance to be covered was great. The "Dark and Bloody Ground" was overrun with savage war parties, and the exact whereabouts of the surveyors unknown. Nonetheless, Daniel and Stoner succeeded. They were back in the Clinch Valley within sixty-one days, having raced eight hundred miles on foot, been undetected by the hostile Indians, and reached all of the scattered surveying parties in time to warn them of their danger.

Daniel had every reason to be pleased with what he and Stoner had done. Yet, when he had come upon James Harrod and seen him and his thirty-four men laying out lots and building cabins at Harrodsburg, Daniel must have regretted that he and his expedition of the year before had been unable to establish the first settlement in Kentucky. Not being a jealous man, he bore no grudge. Instead, he helped briefly with the surveying and even built a rough cabin.

On his return to the Clinch Valley, Daniel found that the war on the frontier, known to history as Lord Dunmore's War, had already reached the fighting stage. It came to its climax at Point Pleasant on October 10, 1774. There, on the heights looking down on the Great Kanawha River at its junction with the Ohio, a terrible battle took place. It was the bloodiest in Virginia's long history of conflicts with the Indians and one of the bloodiest ever fought by white men and Indians for possession of the continent.

From dawn until almost dusk a force of 1,100 backwoodsmen, ably commanded by Andrew Lewis, opposed a thousand braves no less ably commanded by Chief Cornstalk, a famous Shawnee leader. At the end of a day of fierce hand-to-hand fighting between foes equally matched in courage and almost equally matched in numbers, the Indians retreated. They fled only because they mistook a rearrangement of some of Lewis' men for the approach of Lord Dunmore with reinforcements.

Although the Indian losses were heavy and included some of their best warriors, by sundown the number of white men killed or wounded was double that of the enemy. Even so, the white men won the day, and by winning it hastened the end of Lord Dunmore's War.

Daniel had tried to enlist in Lewis' army as soon as he came back from his dash into Kentucky to warn the surveyors. To his disappointment he was told that he could best serve by raising a company to protect the Clinch Valley, which was in constant danger of attack. Chief Logan himself was among the attackers. He had not forgotten his vow. The presence of Logan and his braves, who ambushed and killed three of Daniel's men, indicates that Daniel, though not with Lewis' army where he had wanted to be, was doing a risky and needed job. His neighbors knew his value and were grateful to him. They petitioned to have him made a captain.

As Captain Boone, Daniel was released from the militia in November. A few months later he celebrated his freedom from public duties by hunting alone in Kentucky again. His days, however, of being in Kentucky as a lonely hunter were almost over.

On his next trip in the spring Daniel went as the leader of thirty men. They were all employed by Richard Henderson in a land development project Henderson had organized and named the Transylvania Company. Their task was to open up the wilderness for others by cutting a road and establishing a settlement.

Henderson and Daniel had been friends for many years in the Yadkin Valley. Henderson may even have aided Daniel in raising money for his earlier journeys to Kentucky. In any case he had often listened, his eyes brightening, as Daniel described the wonders of the rich, uninhabited region on the far side of the mountains. These descriptions had burned their way into Henderson's mind. They became the center of his thinking and his planning. That land which Daniel had seen was a land which Henderson himself was determined to see—and settle.

CHAPTER X

THE TRANSYLVANIA
DREAM

RICHARD HENDERSON WAS A REMARKABLE MAN, WELL
educated and prosperous. He had been trained as a law-
yer and had served as a judge. He was able and courageous, too. Instead of frightening him, large plans ex-
cited him. The plan he formed as he thought about
Daniel's stories was both bold and large.

He did not see Kentucky in Daniel's terms. Both men
were interested in having it settled; both wanted land.
But where to Daniel the new country meant freedom,
excellent hunting, and a few neighbors willing to face
many perils, to Henderson Kentucky meant power,
large profits, and a whole series of settlements under
his control. Daniel's was a personal dream; Henderson's
almost imperial. He pictured himself as the founder and
Lord Proprietor of a fourteenth colony.

He was determined to get possession of a huge territory, to keep its largest tracts for himself and his partners, to sell smaller ones to settlers, to charge them for

having these surveyed, to collect rents, and to play a
major part in the government.

Henderson was well aware that he faced legal difficulties. He was defying George III's proclamation about
settling west of the mountains. He had no grant from
the Crown. He was disobeying the laws of both North
Carolina and Virginia, and running the risk of being
called (as he was later) a land pirate.

Nonetheless, Henderson was willing to take the
chance because he knew that certain important factors
were in his favor. He was confident that neither London
nor the colonial governors were in a position to take action against him. He was aware that many colonists
favored what he was doing. Furthermore, he was prepared to make a treaty of his own with the Indians
(though that was also against the law) and thus gain a
title, however vague, to the twenty million acres he
sought to buy from them.

Since the Shawnees to the north had surrendered any
claims they had to Kentucky after the Battle of Point
Pleasant, Henderson called a council of southern tribes.
This was held in March, 1775, at the Sycamore Shoals
on the Watauga River in Tennessee. Daniel helped
assemble there some 1,200 Cherokee leaders to meet the
managers of the Transylvania Company.

The frontiersmen had their rifles with them as they
faced the wide semicircle of painted Indians. Henderson
addressed these braves with all the eloquence he had.

The offer he made the Cherokees sounded generous. For their hunting grounds he agreed to pay them $50,000 worth of ornaments, guns, utensils, cloth, and clothing.

A chief named Dragging Canoe, who hated the whites as much as he hated giving up a territory his people had long thought theirs, opposed the transaction. When he warned his hearers that a dark cloud hung over the land, he spoke with a prophet's tongue. Few red men listened to him, however, and fewer whites.

Tempted by Henderson's offer, the Cherokees signed the treaty and were satisfied until the goods were distributed. They then discovered to their sorrow and anger how much they had given away for so little in return. A brave rightly pointed out that in a single day's hunting he could have shot enough deer to buy the one shirt which he received as his share of the payment for these lands.

The Indians had made a bad bargain, the Transylvania Company a good one. It looked as if Henderson's bold plan would triumph. But Henderson, bright as he was, had made a fatal mistake. He was no rascal; he was merely out of step with his times.

He was organizing the Transylvania Company on much the same lines he would have followed had he been establishing a Crown Colony a hundred and fifty years before. The powers he dreamed of for himself were those of one of the earlier Royal Proprietors.

The same Henderson who had outwitted the Indians had failed to consider the changed thinking of his fellow colonists. He did not realize that settlers were anxious to cross the mountains in their search for freedom. More important still, he seemed unaware that freedom itself was a gale blowing up and down the coast and about to turn into that hurricane, the American Revolution.

Henderson had learned nothing from the tax-hating "Regulators" in North Carolina who, when he was a judge, had driven him out of his own courtroom. Apparently he had not noticed the rising fury against King George III and his stubborn ministers. He shared both their deafness and their blindness.

"Taxation without representation" was a phrase which seems not to have reached his ears. Although some tea had been dumped into Boston's harbor fifteen months before the Sycamore Shoals council, the meaning of those scattered tea leaves appears to have escaped Henderson. He understood that the governors of North Carolina and Virginia were too weak to take action against him, but obviously he did not understand why.

Many colonists who had been loyal subjects of his Britannic Majesty were recognizing a new loyalty. They were beginning to think of themselves as Americans. The hour for the Minute Men had struck. Up and down the seaboard angrier and angrier protests were being

Angry protests were being heard

heard. The war fever was rising, the New World readying itself to be independent of the Old.

The First Continental Congress had already met. During the same month that the meeting was held at Sycamore Shoals, Patrick Henry was echoing the growing sentiment of many of his countrymen in his cry, "As for me, give me liberty, or give me death!" A month after Henderson's speech to the Cherokees the hoofbeats of Paul Revere's horse and those shots at Lexington and Concord would be heard round the world. Three months later George Washington, whose interest in Kentucky lands was almost as great as that of the founder of the Transylvania Company, would have left Virginia for Massachusetts to take command of the Continental Army under an elm in Cambridge.

The American Revolution was approaching at a gallop. But Henderson continued to treat liberty and individual rights as if they were still locked in their stalls. The services Henderson performed for Kentucky with his company were outstanding. He hastened the whole process of settling. There was nothing villainous about his project. It was brave and daring. Yet from the outset the Transylvania Company was doomed to a short life by public events and private feelings which Henderson either misread or overlooked.

Even before the treaty with the Cherokees was signed, Henderson had started Daniel and his thirty men on their way to Kentucky. With their axes swinging, they were already hard at work, blazing and cutting that famous path, the Wilderness Road, over which thousands were to travel.

From Powell's Valley Daniel and his party passed through the Cumberland Gap, coming upon the old Warriors' Path which they widened and cleared of underbrush. Thereafter, they followed at different times two clearly marked buffalo traces. They then slashed their way through twenty miles of brush. Finally, on the 6th day of April, 1775, they reached their destination. It was Big Lick, just below the mouth of Otter Creek on the bank of the Kentucky River.

As a hunter, Daniel had seen this valley before. Now he saw it as a settler. And, as settlers, he and his men began to clear the bottom lands and chop down the trees to build that huddle of cabins, the capital of Transylvania, which was to be known as Boonesborough.

Daniel and his group had had their difficulties on the way. In the last days of their journey Indians had attacked them, killing one man and wounding two more. Nonetheless, they had reached their goal. Once there, they set about the rugged work which had to be done.

Naturally they rejoiced when two weeks later Henderson came driving up with several wagons loaded with goods and tools and with a party of his own. For a while Daniel and his men forgot both their labors and their worries. Their road had proved passable. Their settle-

Daniel and his men were hard at work,

blazing and cutting the Wilderness Road

ment seemed to be safe because of the reinforcements Henderson brought with him. They were happy and showed their pleasure by saluting the new arrivals with a running fire of about twenty-five "guns."

CHAPTER XI

THE STORM BREAKS

THOSE WELCOMING GUNS HAD BEEN FIRED IN APRIL. In September they were heard again in Boonesborough. This time it was Daniel who came towards the cabins, and he did not come alone. Rebecca was with him. So was his family. And so were twenty men.

Daniel had gone back to get Rebecca in June. Being Rebecca, she had come with him as soon as she could. She had brought her three sons and four daughters with her and the few crude things she owned with which to equip her home. Daniel had told her for years about the wonders of Kentucky. But what Rebecca thought when she said good-by to her neighbors, what she thought as she traveled three hundred miles through the lonely wilderness, and what she thought when she first saw the untidy little cluster of cabins where she was now to live, no one knows.

It is not hard to guess what the men who had built those cabins thought when they saw Rebecca and Daniel's family coming to join them. A place fit for women and children was no longer a camp. It was a settlement,

a real settlement, meant to last—the beginning of a
town.

In no time other families followed. Squire Boone
brought his. The Calloways came with their two daughters. The secret door in the mountains had been pried
open; the westward movement had begun in earnest.
By the end of the first year more wives had arrived with
their growing sons and daughters.

Boonesborough was not the only goal of the men,
women, and children who traveled over the Wilderness
Road or came down the Ohio. There were by now three
other settlements within the lands Henderson had purchased. There was the outpost, or "station," which Benjamin Logan had built to the south at St. Asaph. There
was another small station at Boiling Spring. Largest and
oldest was Harrodsburg, some fifty miles to the west of
Boonesborough. James Harrod had laid it out the year
before, and had returned to it with a hundred men at
the end of Lord Dunmore's War.

The people in these three settlements had no liking
for Henderson's Transylvania Company or the kind of
government he wanted to set up. They doubted if his
treaty with the Cherokees really entitled him to the
vast tract he claimed as his. Since they had reached it
first, and built on it, they thought the land was theirs.
The fact that there were more of them than there were
of Henderson's followers gave them a feeling of strength
which added to their sense of being right. This did not
make things easy or comfortable for Henderson.

In the next few years other settlements would be started in Kentucky within and far beyond Transylvania. Some of these were to be abandoned during the coming war. Several were to take root. All were to face the terror of Indian attacks. Most of the men and women who came—and had the hardihood to stay— were of Scotch-Irish stock. They were a resolute group, determined to fight for their new homes at the risk of being murdered or scalped.

They were people like the Boones, the Bryans, the Calloways, the Logans, and the Floyds. They were people like the McAfees, the Hites, the Bowmans, the Bullitts, the McClellans, the Todds, the Bledsoes, and the Lewises. They all knew Daniel, and some of them were his closest friends. Their courage was huge, their characters strong as hickory. By choosing to do what they did, they showed that they had in them the stuff of heroism. Doubtless they would have smiled had anyone told them this. They had always lived with danger and, therefore, took it for granted.

Among them were some who became national heroes. One of these was the famous scout and Indian fighter Simon Kenton, whose bravery and quick-wittedness can be measured by what he did one April day in 1778 to save Daniel's life. When the Shawnees were attacking Boonesborough, as they were fond of doing, he and Daniel had gone out with a party and been ambushed. Daniel had fallen to the ground, his ankle shattered by a bullet. Just as the warrior who had fired it was about

to tomahawk Daniel, Kenton shot him and, fighting off other Indians, made a dash for the fort carrying Daniel on his back.

Among these early settlers was George Rogers Clark, that brave and colorful figure who was to emerge during the Revolution as America's outstanding military leader on the frontier. He, too, knew Daniel and in the coming years would get to know him better under the tests of battle.

It was Clark who was to organize a militia in Kentucky. It was he who was to carry the war into the enemy-held territories to the north and seize the English forts on the Mississippi at Cahokia and Kaskaskia. Above all, it was he who was to take Fort Vincennes, and then retake it by a brilliant march across swamps in icy weather, forcing its redcoated garrison to surrender in February, 1779. It was he who captured there Henry Hamilton, the British lieutenant-governor known to frontiersmen as "the hair-buyer," because of the good money he was supposed to pay Indians for American scalps.

If at the time of Rebecca's arrival at Boonesborough people were on the move, so were events, and far more swiftly. When the storm of the American Revolution broke, it struck Kentucky as hard as it did the seaboard. No cabin door could be shut against the gale; no stockade was safe from its fury. The British under Hamilton made certain of this. Needing allies, they did everything they could to stir up the Indians against the Americans and send them on the warpath once more.

When this happened and the massacres in the wilderness began to multiply, many settlers were frightened. They were unwilling to stay in a land where any day or night painted warriors might batter down their doors and carry off their scalps. These weaker ones hurried back across the mountains, leaving only the iron-willed behind.

During one desperate winter the number of people in

Kentucky dwindled to a mere two hundred. The importance to the American fight for independence of this small group, and of those who came to reinforce them, cannot be overestimated. They formed a line of defense which kept the back door to the southern colonies closed on Indians and British alike.

Henderson's plans did not escape the storm. Its lightning put a quick end to his Transylvania Company. Shortly after his arrival at Boonesborough, Henderson held a congress near the cabins under a great elm. His hope was to establish a government—*his* government—at this meeting and to win men like Harrod and Logan to his side. Among the speakers was Daniel. As might be expected, he did not discuss law or politics. He urged that a bill be passed to preserve game.

Henderson went so far as to announce a second congress for the next year. This meeting was never held. By 1776 the Transylvania Company was having its serious troubles.

Although Henderson tried to gain the support of the Continental Congress and the Virginia Legislature, neither of these bodies approved of his Transylvania project. They knew the military value of the lands to the west. They knew the British had forts in Detroit and along the Mississippi. They knew the English would have little trouble persuading the Indians to go to war. They knew a militia was needed to defend the frontier, and that men fighting for freedom would not fight for a colony largely owned and run by one man.

The arguments they listened to were the very sensible ones of such men as Harrod and George Rogers Clark who, for the safety of all concerned, asked that Kentucky be made a county of Virginia.

This action was taken. Kentucky County was formed, and two years later the Transylvania Company was declared illegal. The valuable work Henderson and his partners had done in opening up her new county was not forgotten, however, by Virginia. As thanks they were granted two hundred thousand acres in Kentucky.

Henderson had intended, after the cutting of the Wilderness Road and the founding of Boonesborough, to express his gratitude to Daniel by giving him two thousand acres. But, in the process of Kentucky's becoming a part of Virginia and the Transylvania Company's being put out of business, Daniel never received his present. Although he was disappointed, the long fierce struggle of the Revolution left him little time to grieve over the reward that should have been his.

The Cherokee chief who had said a dark cloud hung over the land had been right. How right, the pioneers in Kentucky would come to know during the next seven years, and none more completely than Daniel and his family.

CHAPTER XII

AN EVENTFUL
SUNDAY

SUMMER IS A FRIENDLY AND RELAXING TIME. ITS greens are soft as cushions; its colors gay and party-like. Its lazy heat is comforting. When its days are sun-drenched everything seems at peace, and peace seems to be everywhere.

On the 17th of July, 1776, even Boonesborough had a peaceful look. That it was Sunday only added to the calm. The past few months had been tranquil enough. Those Indian massacres, which had sent so many frightened settlers back across the mountains, had taken place in the cold, leafless weeks of December. They now seemed a long way off, almost as far away as the red-coated armies on the coast.

As was proper on the Sabbath, there had been a reading of the Bible in the morning. As was no less proper for an older man on a Sunday afternoon, Daniel, sleepy from his midday meal, had gone to his cabin to take a nap. After he had removed his moccasins and before he dozed off, it perhaps crossed his mind that the stockade,

86

which by connecting the cabins would turn Boonesborough into a fort, had not been completed. The stockade ought to be finished. He knew that. Yet on such a lolling summer's day surely it could wait.

The sun, which had added to Daniel's drowsiness, kept the young people out-of-doors. They were playing by the river. Among them was Daniel's daughter Jemima, whose shouts and laughter her father may have dimly heard before he went to sleep.

Jemima had two friends with her, the Calloway sisters—Betsey, who was sixteen and Fanny, who, like Jemima, was fourteen. The three girls decided to go out in the settlement's only canoe. When they had drifted downstream about a quarter of a mile, they saw beyond a clump of bushes on the far bank some flowers they wanted to pick. While trying to land, they lost control of their boat.

They did not suspect that in the bushes, towards which the Kentucky's current carried them, five Indians were hiding. These Indians had been watching the canoe, hoping this very thing would happen. At the right moment they plunged into the water and dragged the screaming and struggling girls ashore. They then silenced them by threatening to kill them and hurried them through a ravine up and over a hill.

Some say the girls were not missed until milking time, others that their screams were heard in Boonesborough and that Daniel, on hearing them, jumped up, grabbed his rifle, and raced to the river, more alarmed than his neighbors had ever seen him. He was so upset that he did not realize for hours (and then only when someone pointed it out) that he had not stopped to put on his moccasins.

Pursuing parties were organized at once, one on horseback headed by Colonel Calloway, one on foot led by Daniel. As Daniel advised, Calloway's group did not attempt to follow the Indians. Instead, they galloped north, in order to reach the ford of the Licking River first and stop the red men if they got that far with their

captives. To Daniel and his group fell the task of picking up the trail, shadowing the Indians, and, most difficult of all, overpowering them before they had a chance to kill the three girls.

Daniel found that the trail was not so hard to follow as he had feared. This was due to the courage and ingenuity of the three girls. They did not have Boone and Calloway blood in them for nothing. In spite of being closely watched by the Indians, they managed to give hints of their course by breaking twigs and tearing off and dropping tiny bits of their garments. Each time Daniel and his men came upon one of these markings, their hopes increased. Even so, they were well aware of the difficulties which lay ahead of them and of the dangers faced by the girls.

Daniel realized the braves would become less and less careful the farther they went and the safer they felt themselves to be. The end of the thirty-five-mile chase came at noon and was terrible in its suspense. When the white men crept close to the Indian party, they were delighted to see that the three girls were unharmed. But Daniel and his men knew that one false move by them would cost the girls their lives.

Luckily, the Indians were busy cooking and, therefore, were caught off guard. The frontiersmen took careful aim and fired just as their presence was discovered. Two of the warriors were killed; the other three ran into the canebrake and escaped.

In spite of knives and a tomahawk thrown at the

girls by the departing braves, and John Floyd's mistaking Betsey for a squaw and almost braining her with his rifle butt, the young women were saved. The party that returned them to Boonesborough came back in triumph. They were soon rejoined by Colonel Calloway and his men who, having encountered no Indians, had rightly decided that Daniel must have accomplished his mission.

They had not been home long when exciting news reached the settlement. In distant Philadelphia the Representatives of the United States in General Congress met had pledged their lives, their fortunes, and their sacred honor to support an all-important document. It was to change man's thinking about himself, his rights, and his government. It proved to be what has been called the "birth certificate of a nation." America had made her final break with the British Crown. She had broken a new path, too, and proclaimed her freedom by issuing the Declaration of Independence.

In time the men and women in the wilderness would know the blessings brought them by this document. For the next few years, however, every cabin on the frontier, including Daniel's, would mainly know the terrors and trials of war and how hard and constant a struggle the fight for liberty always must be.

CHAPTER XIII

CAPTURED BY
THE SHAWNEES

A YEAR AND A HALF AFTER JEMIMA'S CAPTURE, DANIEL was to have his own experiences as a prisoner of the Indians. In the bitter cold of a freezing January he and twenty-nine men had left Boonesborough for the Lower Blue Licks.

They had important work to do. The settlements were in desperate need of salt. In the past it had been sent to them by the seaboard colonies, but the Revolution made the sending of such supplies inconvenient, if not impossible. Fortunately, there was plenty of salt in Kentucky's salt springs or "licks." To prepare it for human use, these waters had to be boiled down in large iron kettles. The pioneers had lacked such kettles until Virginia sent some by pack horse across the mountains. It was with this newly arrived equipment that Daniel and his men went to work.

They had been at the Lower Blue Licks for a month during which, as they worked undisturbed, they had made quantities of salt. They thought their task almost

91

done, and were looking forward to being relieved by another group of salt-makers, when disaster abruptly overtook them.

Towards sundown on the 7th of February Daniel was struggling in a snowstorm to return to camp. He had been out hunting and the horse he led was carrying fresh buffalo meat for himself and his men. Although the horse shied nervously on approaching a fallen tree, Daniel blamed the blinding snow for this. Within a few seconds he knew better. Four Shawnee braves jumped from behind the tree and, though Daniel tried to run away, soon captured him.

The four braves forced Daniel to go with them to their nearby camp. On reaching it he realized at once how serious his situation was. A hundred and twenty warriors were gathered there under Chief Blackfish. With them, dressed and painted like Indians, were James and George Girty, those white traitors to the American cause. Their brother, the even more infamous Simon Girty, would figure darkly in Daniel's life in the coming years.

All the men at the Indian camp had heard of Daniel, all knew the importance of their prisoner. They gave him a loud welcome, shook hands with him, and pretended to greet him as a friend. Among those most pleased to see him were some of the very braves from whom he had escaped eight years before after they had warned him to beware of the stings of the "wasps and yellow jackets." These braves were so delighted to have

him in their power again that they could not help laughing. Daniel, knowing the ways of Indians, fooled them
all into thinking he was as happy to be with them as
they were to have him.

They soon told him their plans. They announced they
were going to attack Boonesborough and wished him to
guide them there. When they added that they expected
Daniel to persuade his group of salt-makers to give
themselves up before the expedition started, they presented Daniel with one of the most difficult decisions he
ever had to reach. To make a choice affecting his own
life was easy enough; to make one which affected so
many other lives was a terrible responsibility.

As he listened to the Indians, the beat of Daniel's
heart may have quickened but the expression of his face
remained unchanged. He thought of Rebecca and the
children. He thought of the men with him and their
families. He remembered that the stockade at Boonesborough was finished only on one side. He realized that,
without his twenty-nine companions and those who
might be coming to relieve them, the defenders of
Boonesborough would be hopelessly outnumbered by
their attackers.

How he could save Boonesborough was Daniel's only
concern. To save it, he knew he must delay the
threatened attack, trust to luck, and sacrifice the few
for the many. To gain time, he went so far as to promise
the Indians that he and his party of salt-makers would
give themselves up and go with them peacefully to their

Daniel used his head as a male

and knocked over several braves

Ohio villages. The Indians in return promised not to hurt their captives.

Daniel pointed out that without attacking Boonesborough they would already have collected a large number of prisoners. He argued that, if the Shawnees went north and stayed there until the snow was gone, their expedition would be far simpler to carry out. It would be better equipped too, because they could buy more arms with the twenty pounds which Governor Hamilton would pay for each American captive delivered alive in Detroit. Daniel, who could play the Indian game as well as any Indian, added as a final inducement that if the Shawnees waited for the spring he would himself guide them to Boonesborough and persuade the settlement to surrender.

The Indians were won over by Daniel's arguments; so were Daniel's men. Though some of the settlers protested sullenly, they admitted the wisdom, both for themselves and their families, of laying down their rifles and going north with the Shawnees.

The red men showed at once how unreliable their promises were. They had guaranteed not to hurt their captives but, now that the white men were helpless, many of the braves were eager to kill them. A council, at which Daniel was allowed to speak, was held to determine their fate.

It lasted for two hours and was presided over by Blackfish, a kindly chief and a man of character who wanted to live up to the agreement. The vote was close

—frighteningly close—but it was accepted as binding. In spite of Blackfish's eloquence, only sixty-one warriors were in favor of sparing the prisoners, while fifty-nine voted to murder them all except Daniel.

After this council the journey to Ohio began. On the way, Daniel was the first to be forced to run the gauntlet. Running the gauntlet was the odd ritual of torture with which Indians welcomed their prisoners. To red men it was at once a test and a game. It was their way of learning which were the weaklings and which the strong.

They would stand in two rows on either side of a line, and, armed with sticks, stones, antlers, or tomahawks, beat the man who ran between them. Only the hardiest survived, and often these suffered permanent injuries. Since the Indians considered this a sport, they were as willing to cheer their victims as to destroy them. Daniel won their admiration by zigzagging down the course at great speed, using his head as a mallet and knocking over several braves, to the delight of the others, and coming out of the ordeal with only a few bruises.

CHAPTER XIV

CHIEF BLACKFISH'S "SON"

THE TRIP NORTH WAS UNCOMFORTABLE, THE WINTER uncommonly cold. Little or no game was found. Often the shivering party had nothing except slippery elm bark to chew on. Every night the prisoners were tied up and watched by guards. Many of the white men grumbled; but not Daniel. His fellow salt-makers were amazed to see how cheerful he was, how much he joked and laughed, and how happy he seemed to be. The more experienced of them understood the trick he was playing, and played it too. There were others who refused to follow Daniel's example and even began to doubt his loyalty.

After passing through several villages, the Shawnees led their captives to their largest town, Little Chillicothe. The Indians there were overjoyed at such a sizeable catch of Americans. They were surprisingly friendly, too; so friendly that Daniel and at least sixteen of his group, who pretended to be contented, were solemnly adopted into the tribe.

Adoption was an old Indian custom. More than being an act of forgiveness, it was, especially if the prisoners were young men or boys, a sensible method of getting recruits. By means of it families that had lost their sons in battle gained new sons. These were chosen from the captives who were best behaved and most courageous. Once it was clear that a prisoner would not try to escape, a warrior would take him into his wigwam, treating him with as much affection as if he were really a member of the family.

Glad as they were to have their lives spared, neither Daniel nor his men can have enjoyed the ceremony of being adopted. It took a long time and had its embarrassing features. What was worse, it hurt.

According to one of his early biographers, who had talked often with Daniel, the hair of the man being adopted was plucked out until only a tuft some three or four inches in diameter was left on the crown of his head. This scalp lock was then cut, tied with ribbons, and decorated with feathers. Next the candidate would be undressed and led, usually by squaws, to a river or stream where he would be washed and rubbed "to take all his white blood out." Thereafter, when he had scrambled into his clothes, he would be escorted to the council-house. The chief would make a welcoming speech, the new brave's face and head would be fashionably painted, and what the Indians considered a feast would be served.

When he was plucked and painted in this fashion,

Daniel was a Shawnee. At least, he was outwardly. He was fortunate in having as his new "father" no less a person than Blackfish himself, whose attention he had attracted from the first. The chief became genuinely fond of Daniel and so did his squaw. They called him Sheltowee, meaning Big Turtle, and looked upon him with pride as their son.

To Daniel, as to his men, it seemed the winter months would never end. The wigwams were cold, smoky, and drafty. They were dirty, too, and filled with fleas and bedbugs. The food, consisting of beans, pumpkins, dried corn, hominy, and game, was neither pleasant to look at nor easy to swallow, since often all of these would be dumped into one kettle and boiled until they became a greasy mess.

In spite of such hardships and the inner worry he knew, Daniel gave the appearance of being happy. When he was allowed to hunt, he brought what he had killed home to his red "father." If he found himself in a shooting contest with some Shawnees, he remembered the lesson he had learned long ago in the Yadkin. He shot well enough to show his skill but never well enough to make his rivals jealous.

If Daniel laughed, talked, and whistled a lot, he also listened. Little by little, from hints dropped here and there, he pieced together the plans being made for the attack on Boonesborough in the coming spring. He also kept his sharp eyes open, noting every detail of the countryside through which he passed. Mostly he waited, wondering if the chance would ever come for him to escape, and hoping it would come before it was too late.

The Indians continued to be proud of having so many white prisoners. What they counted a triumph Daniel was later to say was an error. He thought the Shawnees never made a greater mistake than when, by taking white men into the heart of their country, they enabled their captives to learn the exact locations of their villages and the paths leading to them. In the avenging years ahead, when American forces were to sweep through this Indian country under such leaders as Anthony Wayne and George Rogers Clark, burning these villages and destroying crops, Daniel was to be proved correct.

That was in the future. For the moment the Indians had it their way, and their way was not easy for Daniel. Often he had to bite his lower lip hard not to lose his self-control. He suffered acutely whenever he saw some of his own men—his Boonesborough neighbors and friends—beaten without mercy or compelled to run the gauntlet because of having shown their hatred of their captors.

A few of the victims of these tortures looked at Daniel with accusing eyes, not realizing what he was doing and beginning to believe he was a traitor. Daniel read their thoughts and understood their feelings. Nonetheless, he continued to play his game, reminding himself with all the strength he had that what mattered most to him and to these men was Boonesborough, which must be warned and strengthened in time.

Early in March, 1778, Blackfish decided to go to Detroit. He wanted to see Henry Hamilton, the British lieutenant-governor there, and to sell him those surly Americans no Indians wished to adopt.

Blackfish took his new "son" along with his party, and Daniel saw face to face the man who, rightly or wrongly, was hated and feared up and down the frontier as the "hair-buyer." Hamilton, realizing how valuable Daniel could be to the English cause, treated him with respect. He showed him many courtesies, not guessing that Daniel was fooling him just as he had fooled the Shawnees.

The governor was surprised and delighted to have Daniel produce from the leather bag he wore around his neck the captain's commission he had been issued when he served with the British colonial forces in Lord Dunmore's War. Daniel carried this commission because he knew that Indians, if ever they caught him, would be impressed by a document which established him as an officer in the army of their British allies.

Hamilton was no less impressed. He was the more convinced of Captain Boone's loyalty to the Crown when Daniel said he would undertake to persuade the citizens of Boonesborough to surrender and follow him back to Detroit. This offer pleased Hamilton to such an extent that he attempted to obtain Daniel's liberty by offering to pay Blackfish a hundred pounds for him. Blackfish, however, refused to let him go, insisting he was too fond of his new "son" to lose him.

Even when Blackfish and his party prepared to leave the fort at Detroit, Hamilton's kindnesses to Daniel continued. As a farewell present he gave Daniel a pony, saddle, bridle, blanket, and some silver trinkets. The truth is Hamilton was so taken in that on telling Daniel good-by he talked to him about his duty to *their* Most Gracious Majesty, King George III.

When he got back to Little Chillicothe, Daniel saw at once that the long-discussed plans for attacking Boonesborough were becoming definite. The village had changed. It had lost its peaceful winter look and was an armed camp. The air was heavy with talk of war, and signs of the war's coming were everywhere. The beat of the tom-toms had quickened. They now pounded like the hearts of angry men. Runners were being sent out to race from town to town with the war pipe. Each day strange Mingos, Delawares, and Shawnees were appearing, impatient and prepared for action.

This different feeling and these different conditions did not make life easier for Daniel and the other adopted Americans. Adding to their troubles were things which had happened both during and after Blackfish's visit to Detroit. While the chief was there, one of the shrewdest of the pioneers, a man named Johnson who since his capture had pretended to be a half-wit, escaped. He was the first to reach Kentucky with news of the coming invasion and details as to the whereabouts of the Shawnee villages.

In May this same Johnson led a small raid against one of these Ohio towns. As proofs of his success, he came home with some stolen horses and a sickening number of Indian scalps. Early in June some other men from Boonesborough made a similar surprise attack on another village, collecting many horses and killing several Shawnees.

The Indians were angered and alarmed by these expeditions. Since they felt they could no longer trust their white "sons," they began to guard them more closely. As the days crept by, Daniel, though he continued to smile, flamed with impatience. It began to look as if his chance would never come. Then, unexpectedly on the 16th of June, it did come, and in a way that must have made Daniel laugh.

This time it was the Indians who needed salt. Some braves had gone to make it at the salt springs of the Scioto. Their leader was Blackfish, who had brought Daniel with him. According to one story, the Shawnees were hard at work and keeping, as usual, a watchful eye on Daniel. The day would have passed like all those other days of captivity, had not such a tremendous flock of wild turkeys suddenly filled the sky that, for a moment, the Indians forgot about Daniel.

Such a moment was all Daniel needed and all he had been praying for. He dashed for the woods and disappeared, and kept on dashing for the next four days.

Daniel dashed for the woods and disappeared

During those four days Daniel, who was now forty-four, covered a hundred and sixty miles and had only one meal, some meat from a buffalo he killed at the Blue Licks. Although exhausted and half-starved when he approached the little group of cabins for which he had been heading, he did not care. He had reached Boonesborough. In time, he hoped.

CHAPTER XV

A SUMMER
OF SUSPENSE

DANIEL HAD AN IMMEDIATE DISAPPOINTMENT WHEN
he reappeared, as if from the grave, after his four-and-
a-half months of captivity. Jemima, now married to
Flanders Calloway, was still in the settlement. His
brother Squire was there, too. But Rebecca was not.
She had waited, hoping and fearing as the weeks
lengthened into months. Then she had given up hope.
Convinced that Daniel was dead, she had returned in
despair to the Yadkin with her family. It had seemed
the wisest thing to do, and Daniel understood.

His first desire was to go to Rebecca and his children.
One look around him told him that, before he could do
so, a great deal had to be done, and done at once, to
ready Boonesborough for the expected siege. In spite of
having been warned that the Indians were planning to
attack, the settlement was in no condition to defend
itself.

The log palisade connecting the cabins was not finished. The two gates needed to be strengthened. The

blockhouses at the four corners of the rectangular-shaped fort had not been completed. The land around the stockade was still thick with underbrush which offered the enemy protection. No less serious, the settlers continued to depend for water on springs outside the walls and had done nothing about digging a well inside the protected area.

Daniel changed all this. The palisade was finished in

ten days. The blockhouses were completed. Rain barrels were put out. A new well was started. An attempt was made to cut away the underbrush. Furthermore, a request was forwarded to Virginia, asking for reinforcements within six weeks. Both Logan's Station and Harrodsburg were persuaded to help by sending the few men they could spare.

A long, tense period of waiting followed. It was a period of wondering if war whoops instead of cockcrows would greet the sun. The settlers peered through the morning mists to see if painted warriors were lurking in the forests beyond the clearing. By day they listened for the sudden crack of rifles. When they ventured beyond the stockade to water and feed the cattle, gather vegetables, or shoot game, they never knew if their scalps were safe.

Some good news heartened the waiting men and women. Word came that the English outposts at Kaskaskia, Cahokia, and Vincennes had fallen to George Rogers Clark, and that the French King had sent a fleet to aid the American Revolutionists in their fight against Britain. Although the good news helped, it did not outweigh the bad.

Other prisoners who had escaped from the Shawnees reported that the large Indian force, which Daniel had seen gathering, was moving against Boonesborough. This added to the suspense, as did the fact that after Daniel's return six weeks dragged by and still no Indians appeared. There were those who began to argue that perhaps the whole invasion had been called off. They reasoned that Blackfish, knowing the settlement had been warned, would not risk attacking it when it had had time to prepare itself for a siege.

Daniel could not bear either the waiting or the uncertainty. Towards the end of August he determined to go out with a party and find out what the Indians were up to. Some questioned the wisdom of such a move. They said it would dangerously reduce the small number of Boonesborough's defenders. No one looked with graver disapproval on the plan than Colonel Calloway. Remembering the stories about how happy Daniel had been among the Indians and his offer to surrender the settlement, the Colonel started to doubt Daniel's loyalty.

Doubts or no doubts, Daniel set forth. His party crossed the Ohio River and pushed into the country from which he had recently escaped. Since he did not at first meet Blackfish's forces, Daniel could not know that, as he was going north, the Indians were heading south. He and his scouts, however, did observe that in the villages they spied on there were only old men and no young braves. This led them to conclude that the invaders must be already on the warpath.

How right they were, they discovered on the 5th of September after they had been out a week. When they were on their way back and were a short distance from home, they came across a force of more than four hundred Indians and some French-Canadians which Blackfish was leading against Boonesborough. Unobserved by the enemy, Daniel's party crept past and hurried to the settlement, reaching it the next day.

On learning of the nearness of the Indians, the men, women, and children in the fort all joined in the rush of final preparations. Every pot and barrel was filled with water. Rifles were cleaned, bullets molded, some of the cattle brought in, food cooked, and the defenses given a last grim inspection. When night fell, fires were lighted in every cabin and work continued. It was the kind of long-short or short-long night (who can say which?) known to those expecting battle the next day. Yet once again the sun rose on a peaceful valley, with no Indians in sight.

CHAPTER XVI

TEN DAYS
OF TERROR

IT WAS NOT UNTIL TEN THAT MORNING THAT THE RED men appeared. They came openly over the hill, carrying the British flag, and halted beyond the range of rifle fire. A messenger advanced to the fort, waving a white banner, and asked for Daniel. He reminded Daniel of his promise to surrender Boonesborough. Adding that Blackfish was anxious to have a talk with his "son," he suggested that Daniel go with him to see the chief.

Although the danger was great, the log gate was opened and Daniel went out alone. As they watched him leave, many of the settlers were certain they would never see him alive again. But, regardless of the risk he took and was to ask others to take by meeting with the Indians, Daniel was once more playing for time. He still hoped the reinforcements from Virginia would arrive at any moment. He therefore welcomed conferences which would postpone action.

Blackfish seemed as friendly as ever. He greeted Daniel with affection. His smiles were interrupted only when he wept at the thought that his dear "son" had ever run away from him. He acted as if he believed Daniel were going to live up to his agreement, and produced a letter from Governor Hamilton. In it Hamilton urged the pioneers to give themselves up and go in peace to Detroit. He promised that if they did they would not be punished for having fought against Great Britain.

This meeting between Daniel and Blackfish was the first of several conferences during the next anxious hours. The people within the fort, though outnumbered at least six to one, were determined to fight rather than accept Blackfish's terms. Luckily, the attackers did not know how few defenders there were in Boonesborough. They had been misled by the exaggerated figures given them by their white prisoners.

They were further misled by a very simple trick. This was to have the women inside the stockade dress up as men and keep walking past the open gate where they could be seen by the Indians watching from a distance. Even dummies are said to have been dressed up in the same way and placed around the palisade so that their heads could be counted.

The attitude of the Indians was friendly at first. When it became clear that the white men might be fooling them, their temper changed. At the final conference they resorted to some trickery of their own.

Before this meeting, Blackfish had insisted on being attended by eighteen braves. Daniel did not dare to

weaken Boonesborough by bringing that many of its
defenders with him. Accompanied by eight unarmed
settlers, he met the chief within gun range of the fort,
having agreed with the riflemen inside that they would
fire if any trouble occurred.

For a while the conference seemed to go smoothly.
Both the settlers and the Indians pretended to want
peace. As the meeting was drawing to a close, the moment came for everyone to shake hands. After this was
done, Blackfish pointed out that each of the nine white
men should join hands with two braves, in order to
make peace doubly sure. Although Daniel suspected
a trick, there was nothing he could do. As soon as the
white men extended their hands, the Indians grabbed
the settlers and tried to drag them away as prisoners.

A general scuffle followed, which turned into a dangerous fight. Colonel Calloway was the first to get away.
Daniel broke loose from Blackfish and knocked him
down. The other men, including Squire Boone, also
shook off the braves who held them. Meanwhile the
riflemen in the fort fired, as did the main body of the
Indians who had been watching from a distance. During
the skirmish Daniel received two slight wounds and
Squire was shot in the shoulder. Although the settlers
found themselves running through a cloudburst of bullets and hurled tomahawks and knives, they managed
to reach the stockade.

The siege of Boonesborough now began in earnest. It
was the fiercest of the many sieges known to Kentucky,

and the longest. For ten terrible days and nights, from
the 8th to the 17th of September, 1778, it tested the
character and ingenuity of the attackers no less than of
the defenders.

The Indians had more in their favor than vastly su-
perior numbers. The formation of the land aided them.
At Boonesborough, as at some of the other settlements,
the pioneers had not been wise in choosing a site for
their fort. The stockade was surrounded by hills from
which the enemy could see what was going on and create
confusion by firing stray shots at those inside the walls.
The red men were also able to find useful cover outside
the fort in the underbrush, which had not been cut away
entirely in spite of Daniel's urging.

All the advantages were not on the Indians' side. The
settlers, caught in a trap, could not retreat and would
not surrender. Knowing what their fate would be if they
failed, they fought with the frenzy of those fighting for
their lives. They had had time to prepare. Their system
of loopholes and blockhouses was good. Their stockade
not only offered them protection but, by allowing them
to shoot without being seen, made up in part for their
lack of numbers.

At the beginning of the siege the Indians were per-
plexed and scared by a wooden cannon which Colonel
Calloway had rigged up. It made a lot of noise and until
it burst, which it soon did, it may even have killed a
few braves.

The Indians attempted to take the fort by every

means of warfare known to them. Their gunfire was incessant and maddening. They wore down the defenders by granting them no sleep. They made the days hideous by firing on the cattle in the stockade, causing them to stampede and bellow in their fright.

Time after time, the Indians tried to scale the walls, only to be shot down or driven away by the pioneers who had their rifles trained on them. Again and again, while splitting the air with war whoops, the attackers threw flaming faggots at the cabins. The cabins would have burned had not almost nightly rains put out the fires. The red men even dug a tunnel from the river toward the stockade. They were on the point of reaching it and blowing up the fort when the dampness of the earth caused their tunnel to cave in.

The chances of the settlers' being able to hold out were always slight and often seemed hopeless. Supplies were running low and tempers short. After a week had passed, many of the pioneers, who were willing to face the ugly facts, must have thought they could not last much longer.

Yet somehow they endured the mounting hardships of the eighth, the ninth, and the tenth days. When the sun rose on the eleventh morning, the men and women of Boonesborough looked out from the fort with unbelieving eyes. There were no Indians to be seen. The woods were blessedly empty and silent.

The first thought of the tired defenders was that the Indians must be playing another trick. They waited a

In vain the Indians tried to scale the walls

few hours inside the stockade, not daring to trust their hopes. Then some scouts slipped out of the fort and returned with the joyful news that Blackfish and his army really had abandoned the siege and were heading for their villages to the north.

The Indian losses had been heavy, thirty-seven dead and many more wounded; the losses of the settlement light, two killed and four wounded. In a fashion that seemed almost miraculous the siege had been withstood and peace, for the moment, had come again. Naturally, there was rejoicing in Boonesborough.

For Daniel the rejoicing did not last long. When the guns were silent, the tongues of gossips began to wag. Men who in private had questioned his loyalty now doubted it in public. There were those like Colonel Calloway who thought that Captain Boone, in the Colonel's phrase, "ought to be broak of his commyssion." They believed he had been guilty of treason both as Blackfish's prisoner and during the siege. They also accused him of being pro-British. They demanded that he face a court-martial.

At the trial Daniel's accusers charged him with leading the Indians, after he had himself been captured, to the camp of his fellow salt-makers and hence being responsible for their being taken prisoners. They thought it strange he had enjoyed the friendship and confidence of Blackfish. They pointed out that Daniel had promised both Blackfish and Governor Hamilton to guide the Indians to Boonesborough, guarantee its surrender, and lead its inhabitants to Detroit where they would live under British rule.

Daniel's detractors also claimed that, after his escape, when he knew the Indians were going to attack any day, he weakened the fort by taking many men with him on a needless scouting party. They further accused him of risking, after the arrival of the enemy, the lives of several of Boonesborough's most valuable officers by having them attend a conference beyond the range of the fort's guns. They maintained he had almost caused the capture or death of these men when, outnumbered two to one, the Indians at their last meeting had grabbed them and attempted to drag them off.

Daniel, who had faced death many times for Boonesborough and who had thought only of how he could serve and save it, was wounded by these charges. They were poor expressions of thanks. But he was grateful for the chance to explain publicly and in detail why he had thought it wisest in each case to do what he had done, and how he had deliberately fooled both the British and the Indians in Boonesborough's interest.

The men who tried him heard Daniel with respect. They knew, as did most of his neighbors, that no one had done so much as he to save Boonesborough. Accordingly, to the delight of nearly everyone in Kentucky, they not only voted to acquit him honorably of every charge but at once promoted him to the rank of major.

With a clear name and a conscience that had always been clear, Daniel headed once again for the Yadkin to join Rebecca and his children at last. The trial cannot have been a pleasant memory for him, however right and happy its outcome. Perhaps it was one reason, when he brought his family back to Kentucky a year later, that he did not choose to settle in the little town named after him, which he had established and for which he had risked his life again and again. There were other reasons. The game was scarcer now. There was less "elbowroom." New people had come and old friends had left.

Daniel had some land about five miles to the northwest of Boonesborough, on the other side of the Kentucky River. With Rebecca, his children, his dogs, and some heavily laden pack horses, he started for it late in 1779. By Boone's Creek and where several buffalo trails crossed, he built a large palisaded cabin, known as Boone's Station. During the coming years he went back to Boonesborough only when he had to or in a time of trouble. Such a time was not too far off.

CHAPTER XVII

WHITE MAN'S CRUELTY

THREE LOGS TIED TOGETHER FLOATED DOWN THE KEN-
tucky River one March day in 1782. Three logs lashed
together and floating down a river would not alarm most
people today. To the sharp-eyed pioneers in Boonesborough, however, who spotted them as they drifted
past the fort, these logs were warnings of troubles to
come.

Since no white men were living upstream, the three
logs, tied together as they were, meant one and only
one thing. Indian war parties were once more on the
move. Somewhere above the stockade they were crossing the river on rafts. Summer always found red men
stealing through the Kentucky woods, daubed in their
war paint, turning each cabin into a fort, bringing death
and destruction with them.

If the Indians were earlier than usual this year, it
was due to the mildness of the spring. How many braves
there were or where they would attack, no one could

tell. How many more would threaten the settlements in the months ahead, no one could guess. Daniel and his fellow settlers would learn soon enough, and to their sorrow, in this year which was to prove so costly and decisive that it has been called Kentucky's "year of blood."

Daniel may not have been surprised but he must have been discouraged when he discovered that Indians were again on the warpath. No doubt in the spring he had hoped, along with other frontiersmen, that the coming summer might be different. After all, Cornwallis had surrendered at Yorktown the previous October and Americans everywhere had rejoiced when they heard the news.

Although a formal peace treaty with England had not yet been signed, and was not to be signed until 1783, the hard-fought struggle for independence had been won. Even in Kentucky men, women, and children who had suffered severely during the war years may have felt free at last to dream of peace. But not for long.

North of the Ohio River, in village after village where chiefs and warriors met in council as the winter of 1781-82 crept by, the talk had been of the need for continued warfare. The Indians were quick to realize the dangers they faced because of Britain's defeat.

They knew that more and more Americans were certain now to come streaming across the mountains into their lands. To be sure, Governor Hamilton had been captured at Vincennes by George Rogers Clark and sent to Williamsburg as a prisoner. But the British in Detroit were still able and anxious to help the red men with their raids. If the Indians wanted to drive the Americans out and keep the mountains as their fortress wall, they must act at once.

Blackfish's siege of Boonesborough, though well planned and large-scaled, had been a failure. Future attacks would have to be bigger and based on a different organization. To win, the Indians must fight as they had not fought in the past. Certainly, they must fight as they had not fought in March when that war party (a small one composed only of Wyandots) had crossed the river above Boonesborough. They must not strike tribe by tribe or village by village. They must strike as one, banded together in the kind of confederacy which the great chief Pontiac had once achieved. And strike they did in August in precisely this fashion, under able and ruthless leadership.

When they struck it was against Kentucky, and they were united by two events which had taken place during the spring in Ohio. The first of these filled the Indians with proper hatred, the second with new-found confidence. Since a lot of blood had both times been spilled, more blood was bound to flow in Kentucky that summer. Daniel realized this when he heard the gory details of what had happened in Ohio. He knew too much about Indians not to suspect what was coming—and to dread it.

No incident in the history of the white man's warfare against the red is more shameful to the white men than the Williamson massacre. The Indians at their most savage were never guilty of a greater crime than the one committed against them by Colonel David Williamson and the force of about one hundred Americans who served under him.

In early March these militiamen had pushed from Fort Pitt into Ohio to avenge the recent killing of some borderers by fierce Wyandots.

A detachment of Colonel Williamson's soldiers came upon a group of Delawares, a tribe which had been converted to Christianity by Moravian missionaries. When encountered, these Indians were husking corn in a frozen field. They were as gentle as Christians should be.

The promise given them was that, if they handed over their guns and tomahawks, they would not only know the blessings of peace but would be fed and taken care of by their white brothers. Believing what they were told, thinking that Christians were speaking to Christians, the Delawares meekly surrendered their weapons and followed the militiamen back to the Indian village where Colonel Williamson was waiting.

At first he treated them as friends. Then abruptly he had his soldiers bind their hands and drive the men into one cabin and the women and children into another. When the cabin doors had been barred, Williamson turned to his troops to ask, "Boys, which shall we do, kill them or take them back to Fort Pitt?" Eighty-two of the frontiersmen voted to kill them.

On the following morning Williamson's men divided into two groups and entered the cabins with scalping knives, tomahawks, mallets, and spears. Williamson himself chose the women and children as his victims. While the Indians prayed aloud, the white men slaughtered them without any show of shame or mercy.

One militiaman, seizing a mallet, began his bloody business by crushing the skull of an Indian named Abraham who had the longest hair and hence would yield the finest scalp. This single soldier felled fourteen Delawares before becoming somewhat tired and bored. "My

arm fails me," he said. "Go on in the same way. I think
I have done pretty well."

When the bashing, the beating, the stabbing, and the
scalping were over, the floors of the two cabins were
reddened with the blood and strewn with the bodies of
forty men, twenty women, and thirty-four children.

No wonder the dark forests were soon filled with Indian runners speeding from tribe to tribe to spread the
story of this crime. Or that some braves who in the past
had not wanted to fight were now anxious to go to war.
Yet, horrible as the news was, one Indian leader must
have welcomed it. This was the white man, Simon Girty,
two of whose brothers Daniel had met when he had been
Blackfish's prisoner among the Shawnees.

No chief was more despised by frontiersmen than
this Simon Girty to whom the Williamson massacre was
good news, and none was a better general. Although he
could be kind, as when once he saved Simon Kenton's
life, it is for his brutality that Simon Girty was feared
and is remembered. He was usually referred to by the
settlers as "the white Indian" or "the renegade." There
were even those who so loathed him that they insisted
he had every Christian fault and no savage virtue.

If the white men hated Simon Girty, he, a white man,
hated them with equal heat. For Simon Girty was a
misfit; one of those brilliant men who think themselves
misunderstood and therefore create trouble for themselves and everyone else by going through life nourish-

ing a grudge. Tomahawkings and scalpings, or the screams of men being burned at the stake, held no horrors for Simon Girty. He had known the cruelty of Indians since, in his childhood, first his drunken father and next his worthless stepfather had been butchered by red men.

But Simon Girty liked Indians. He liked their way of life which he had learned when as a captive he had been brought up among the Senecas. He liked their savagery, too, and could be as cruel as the cruelest of them.

After Fort Duquesne had fallen and become Fort Pitt and he had been forced to live there for a while, Simon Girty persuaded himself that he was not properly appreciated by the colonists. When the Revolution broke out and the Americans took over the fort, he slipped away one day with two white men who also felt they were being badly treated.

Simon was determined to get his revenge by working for the British and by living with and fighting for the Indians. To Americans, therefore, he became twice a traitor. They might have understood his siding with the English but they could not forgive his turning Indian.

Simon Girty was wise enough to realize that, if the Indians were to wipe out the settlers and save their lands, they must forget their differences and unite. He had begged them to do this in vain until Colonel Williamson by his crime made many, though not as yet all, chiefs and braves see that Simon Girty was right. Then came the second of the two events of the spring of 1782 which turned Girty's dream of a red man's confederacy into a fact, and cost both Kentucky and Daniel dearly.

CHAPTER XVIII

RED MAN'S TORTURE

Once again the Americans played right into Simon Girty's hands. Instead of being ashamed of Colonel Williamson's butchery, a lot of the frontiersmen were delighted by it. They were certain that "the only good Indian was a dead one." Having killed so many Indians so easily, they were now eager to get on with the work of killing.

Another expedition, consisting of nearly five hundred well-armed and well-mounted men, assembled near Fort Pitt under the command of Colonel William Crawford. Its purpose was to destroy the towns of the Moravian Delawares and Wyandots on the Sandusky River. "No Indian was to be spared, friend or foe; every red man was to die." With such an aim the expedition set out on May 20th.

This time, due to the help given Simon Girty by the Williamson massacre, the Indians were ready. A large number of them attacked the Pennsylvania and Virginia militiamen early in June. In open battle, under skillful leadership and as a unit, they killed or captured the greater part of Colonel Crawford's force and sent the rest running for their lives. As victors, they were as savage as Williamson and his white men had been.

They tomahawked and scalped their prisoners at will, sometimes allowing the women and boys to do this for sport, and in one instance permitting a squaw to cut off a soldier's head and kick it around as if it were a football. Colonel Crawford was himself subjected to the vilest of tortures and, though he died gallantly, was a long time dying.

First they painted his face black, as a sign that he was condemned to death. Then they beat him with sticks or their fists. Next they stripped him and tied him to a stake with a rope just long enough for him to sit down or walk around the post. Then they took their guns and shot some seventy loads of powder into his body from his feet as far up as his neck. After this they cut off his ears.

Soon they set fire to long hickory poles and applied the burning wood to Crawford's naked body which was already black from the gunpowder. Some of the squaws next approached him carrying broad boards upon which they placed flaming coals. They threw these coals on and around him until, in a short time, he had nothing but coals and fire to walk on.

The Colonel turned to Simon Girty, who had been watching these tortures with delight, and begged him to shoot him. Simon Girty's only reply was a laugh—a hideous and fiendish laugh. Thereupon Crawford in his agony prayed to God very quietly, very earnestly. Although he hoped death would deliver him, he continued to stand for almost two hours more when, at last exhausted, he fell down in the ashes on his belly.

How long after this the Colonel lived no one knows. The white man who was forced to watch the torture of his friend, and who after his escape wrote the account of Crawford's death in many of the phrases used here, was at this point led away, supposedly to be killed himself the next day. We do know that Simon Girty "laughed heartily" at such an appalling scene. The frontiersmen soon knew this, too. His laughing did not increase their liking for him.

Simon probably thought that what was done to Crawford and his men was a fair revenge for what had been done by Williamson to the Moravian Indians who believed themselves Williamson's friends. If, however, Simon Girty, the savage, was entertained by Crawford's sufferings, Simon Girty, the gifted leader, was pleased for other reasons.

The Williamson massacre had been a boon to Girty. It had persuaded some tribes and chiefs that he was right in saying they should unite to fight against the Americans west of the mountains. The defeat of Crawford's force came to Girty almost as a present. After it, fear or doubt among the Indians turned to exultation. The defeat of Crawford, like Colonel Williamson's action, was a massacre, but a massacre of the enemy. It

was, therefore, the very kind of victory needed to convince even those chiefs and braves who had held back that they must put away their peace pipes and wage war as one.

Indian honor had been restored; Indian pride was reawakened; Indian hopes rocketed skywards. Pontiac had never won such a battle. Greatness was not a thing of the past. Not since Braddock's defeat had red warriors scored so large a triumph. The fate of Crawford's force had proved that white men could be beaten. The moment to conquer was now. A call for volunteers was, therefore, sent out promptly by Girty and his victorious

chiefs for a large, joint expedition against Kentucky. This time the response was swift and general.

In village after village the war drums began to beat, the war dances were danced, and warriors in their war paint started for the trails leading to the old town of Chillicothe. Shawnees, Cherokees, Wyandots, Miamis, and Pottawattamies were all on the move, racing through the woods. By the first of August, 1782, more than five hundred of them, with many more to come, had found their way to Simon Girty's camp.

When they met in council, Simon Girty spoke to them as an Indian, painted and dressed in their fashion

"Brothers," said he in a speech that throbbed like a war drum in their ears and hearts, "brothers, the Long Knives (the Virginians) have overrun your country and usurped your hunting grounds. They have destroyed the cane, trodden down the clover, killed the deer and the buffalo, the beaver and the raccoon."

"The beaver," he pointed out to the listening Indians who knew he was talking about them rather than beavers, "has been chased from his dam and forced to leave the country. Brothers, was there a voice in the tree of the forest, every part of this country would call upon you to chase away these ruthless invaders who are laying it waste."

With these words and such a purpose quickening their hearts, the Indians started for Kentucky. Their large force included some white rangers and Simon's brothers, George and James. It was headed by two British officers, Caldwell and McKee, who had been sent from Detroit. These officers were in theory the leaders of the invasion. Yet it seems reasonable to assume, on the basis of the tricks employed, the knowledge shown of Indian warfare, and the number of red men from various tribes who were kept under excellent control, that the real leader was Simon Girty.

Certainly, it was a typical Simon Girty touch to drag along some white prisoners to watch the slaughter of their friends and families, and perhaps serve as guides. The Girty touch was also upon the plan itself and the way in which it was carried out.

The expedition moved with such speed and secrecy that it crossed the wide Ohio and pushed far into the enemy country without being observed, and surprised Kentuckians everywhere when its first blow was struck.

Among those surprised was Daniel Boone. Although he had been expecting trouble after the skirmishes of the early spring and summer, even he never guessed that the trouble would be of this size and kind.

CHAPTER XIX

VICTORY
IN DEFEAT

AT THE VERY OUTSET OF THE CAMPAIGN SIMON GIRTY proved how foxlike was his cunning, how brilliant his planning. The target at which he first aimed was not his main one, though, as he intended, the wisest pioneers, including Daniel, were deceived into believing that it was.

Simon knew that when one settlement was attacked other settlements rushed all the men they could spare to its defense. This was the common practice. It was a friendly act and the only way to reinforce a threatened outpost. But it was also dangerous. It meant that forts, already relying on too few defenders, were made the weaker by being stripped of some of these.

Simon had two major objectives—first, Bryan's Station, then, nearby Lexington. Once they had fallen, he felt he would be in a position to take the other settlements in central Kentucky and regain this Blue Grass country for the Indians.

While his main force of six hundred or a thousand warriors (the estimates vary) was advancing undetected towards Bryan's Station, Simon sent seventy Wyandots on a mission as carefully timed as it was misleading. According to schedule, this party on the 10th of August attacked Hoy's Station, a small outpost well to the east and south of the true targets.

When the settlers there saw the size of the Indian party, they thought it must be the major body of attackers which men and women throughout the wilderness frontier had been dreading. This was what Simon had counted on. After doing a little damage and capturing two boys, the Wyandots, also according to plan, began a slow retreat to the north.

Captain Holder and some men from the station were taken in by the trick. They followed the Indians, fought with them, and were compelled to fall back. Immediately, a general alarm was sent from settlement to settlement and volunteers prepared to rush to Hoy's.

The result of the Wyandot raid was exactly what Simon wanted. Most of Kentucky's best riflemen were either advancing or ready to advance—in the wrong direction. When Daniel heard of the attack, he left Boone's Station in other hands and hurried to Boonesborough to lead its garrison against the raiders. Daniel believed he knew where the real danger was. He also knew that within a few days Colonel Benjamin Logan and five hundred men were expected to pass through on

their way north from St. Asaph. He, therefore, felt it
safe to leave both Boone's Station and Boonesborough
almost unguarded.

Simon and his army were meanwhile closing in on
Bryan's Station. Hidden by the darkness, they surrounded the stockade during the night of August 14th
without anyone inside suspecting they were there. The
time of their arrival was important to Simon's plan.
He had calculated that the news of Holder's defeat
would be received early enough on the 14th for a relief
party to leave that same day, thus weakening the defense of the fort and making its capture easy.

Had Simon arrived with his army a few hours later,
had he waited until the middle of the morning of the
15th, his well-thought-out plan would have been the
masterpiece of deception and surprise it came near to
being. He had been right in guessing that Bryan's Station would join the other settlements in rushing aid to
Captain Holder. His only mistake lay in sending out
no advance scouts to tell him when, and if, these reinforcements had left.

At the very moment Simon reached Bryan's Station
feverish preparations were going on inside the fort to
equip a large relief party which was supposed to start
for Hoy's soon after daybreak. This is why, as he crept
forward in the darkness, Simon noticed fires glowing in
each of the forty cabins within the stockade. When he
saw the light from these fires, he assumed that some
runner must have reported Indians were near and that

the few defenders left were struggling to prepare themselves for a hopeless siege.

Although he was to learn better within a few hours,
at sunrise Simon had no way of knowing the number of
the enemy he faced. So far as the settlers were concerned, they were totally unaware that they were about
to be attacked.

They came to sense their danger in ways mysterious
and unexplained. Perhaps a slight skirmish outside the
walls before dawn gave the pioneers their first inkling.
Perhaps at daylight they saw some braves crawling
towards the stockade in the underbrush which had not
been thoroughly cleared away. No one really knows. Yet
somehow the men and women at Bryan's Station did
realize that, instead of being threatened by a small raiding party, they were surrounded by a large force of
Indians.

This is why they sent two men galloping to Lexington
with an appeal for help, hoping that at least one of them
might reach his goal. They were confident that, once the
news reached Lexington, Daniel and Logan would be
notified without delay and hasten to their aid.

Simon had allowed these messengers to pass unop-
posed. He still believed he had surprised the settlement
and did not wish the gunfire of his men to give away
either their presence or their numbers.

The word carried by the messengers spread like wild-
fire from garrison to garrison. It even overtook relief
parties already hurrying to Captain Holder's aid. For-

tunately, it reached Daniel on the night of the 15th before he left Boonesborough for Hoy's. Early the next morning he started for Bryan's Station with a small band, which included his twenty-three-year-old son Israel.

When he rode up to the fort on the afternoon of the 17th, Daniel found to his surprise that the Indians had gone. They had disappeared that morning as suddenly as they had after the long siege of Boonesborough. While scouts were trailing them to determine if they had really withdrawn and reinforcements from Lexington and Harrodsburg were joining those already gathered at Bryan's Station, Daniel heard some of the details of the two-day attack.

He learned how, when a water shortage was discovered soon after the departure of the messengers, the women and girls of the settlement bravely faced death. They had gone out with their buckets to a spring beyond the stockade, pretending not to know that all around them hundreds of Indians were hidden in the bushes. He learned how by skillful deception the forty-two men guarding the station had drawn the fire of the enemy so as to guess at the full size of the attacking force.

Daniel was told that Simon's warriors, when they tried again and again to take advantage of the parching summer heat and set fire to the stockade and the cabins, were prevented from doing so by the accurate shooting of the defenders. He was told that Simon, when he knew his dream of surprise had failed and the siege would be a hard one, had tried to persuade the settlers to surrender. He was pleased to hear that Simon and his braves had been warned to hurry home if they wished to save their scalps, since the whole countryside was marching to the defense of Bryan's Station.

When the scouts returned, they reported there was no question but that the Indians were in full retreat. They had raised the siege and were hastening north by a buffalo trail. A council was held to decide whether they should be followed at once, or whether, considering that the Kentuckians were outnumbered three or five to one, it would not be wiser to wait for the arrival of Colonel Logan and his five hundred men.

Daniel advised waiting. Brave as he was, he was never a man of impulse. He was too wise to be foolhardy, and too experienced to take chances. More than being part of his wisdom, his caution was a proof of it.

Even so, he bowed to the will of most of the one hundred and eighty-one men who, by now, were inside the stockade of Bryan's Station. The majority were for immediate pursuit and Daniel joined them in their expedition.

Every mile they advanced made Daniel the more uncomfortable; every sign he saw made him the more suspicious. Daniel was Indian enough, both by training and in his thinking, to know that retreating warriors do not take pains to mark the path of their retreat unless they wish to be followed.

He did not like the look of the red men's camp which
they passed, with fires left burning and meat untasted.
He did not like the many signs which marked the trail
and invited pursuit. He may not have realized exactly
what Simon and Caldwell were up to. Certainly, he did
not know that, having made one plan based on the trickery of the Wyandot raid, they had been able in the
midst of battle to make another, changing from surprise
to a well ordered direct attack. Certainly, he did not
know that, following the failure of the second plan, they
were now carrying out a third, the most diabolical of the
lot. Nonetheless, Daniel sensed something was wrong.
His every instinct told him so.

After a night's rest the pursuers quickened their speed
and, during the morning of the 19th of August, came to
a horseshoe bend in the Licking River. They saw a few
Indians in full view straggling up the hill on the far
bank towards the nearby Blue Licks.

Clearly, the pioneers had caught up with the enemy.
A second council was held at which Daniel and such
other veteran leaders as Todd, Trigg, and Harlan urged
that the river should not be crossed and a battle risked
until Logan and his men arrived.

Daniel was familiar with this country. He had visited
it on his early trips to Kentucky and come back to it
many times. Near here he and his salt-makers had been
captured by Blackfish. Although scouts reported the hill
on the opposite shore was clear for a mile, Daniel re-

membered that two long ravines over the crest would
supply the enemy with perfect cover for an ambush.

He suggested that the settlers, if they would not wait
for reinforcements, should cross the Licking at a ford
two miles farther up the river. This would lead them to a
more favorable position on higher ground, and avoid the
ravines and the danger of being ambushed.

All of the older and most of the younger officers
agreed with Daniel and recognized the wisdom of his
words. Unluckily, among the many brave frontiersmen
listening to him at the river's edge was Major Hugh
McGary who, though brave, was a fool. He was a pep-
per-brained braggart. His temper was violent, his judg-
ment nonexistent. He was a show-off, capable of great
cruelty and incapable of self-control. He sneered at his
betters, accusing them of being afraid.

"By Godly," he asked, "what have we come here
for?"

"To fight Indians," someone answered.

"By Godly," McGary cried, "then why not fight
them?"

Thereupon, spurring his horse into the river and
brandishing his rifle, he shouted, "All who are not
cowards, follow me, and I'll soon show you the Indians!"

That was enough. It was more than the proud men on
the bank could bear. Ignoring their officers, they followed McGary. Their leaders, including Daniel, were

left with no choice. They, too, plunged their horses into the river and followed. Their one hope was to protect their men by re-establishing some order and giving them a plan.

On reaching the far bank, most of the men dismounted and left their horses untied. A group of twenty-five, including McGary, was sent ahead as an advance party. The others came behind in three long columns. They trudged up the hill and, once the summit was passed, headed for the land between the ravines.

They could not have walked more directly into Simon's well-laid trap, for the ravines, as Daniel suspected, were filled with hidden Indians.

Until the settlers reached the ambush, the silence was heavy and fearful. Then, as quick as thunder and as loud, the Indians opened fire at close range. Of the twenty-five in the advance guard only three men, one of them McGary, survived the first volley.

Within three minutes forty of the settlers were dead or wounded; within five, the battle had become a rout. Instead of being pursuers, the pioneers were now the pursued. To the fearful screech of war whoops they ran for their horses and the river, chased by Simon's braves who by this time had dropped their rifles and were using tomahawks and scalping knives. Everywhere there was hand-to-hand fighting, confusion, and bloodshed.

Many of those wise enough to oppose the attack were among its victims. Harlan fell at the very outset. Trigg was killed, along with nearly all the men from Harrodsburg. Todd, who fought for a while from his white horse after being wounded, soon reeled in his saddle and tottered to the earth.

By the time the short battle had ended, seven of the pioneers had been taken prisoner and sixty-one were left dead on the ground. All the settlements represented at the Blue Licks suffered heavy losses, and grief pushed its way into cabin after cabin.

Although Daniel managed to escape, his son did not. As they were leaving the field among the last, Israel was mortally wounded. He was in agony, his life-blood spilling from him when Daniel picked him up, hoping to carry him to the far shore. He died before the river was reached. After hiding his body, Daniel swam to safety with a sense of being alone which was to stay with him throughout his life.

When Logan's men appeared, Simon and Caldwell decided not to fight them. Although they had lost sixty-five of their braves, the Indians had won what for the moment must have seemed a magnificent victory. Perhaps they hesitated to follow it up because of the size of Logan's force. Or perhaps they feared that General George Rogers Clark might be marching against them with a greater force.

In any case, the Kentuckians met with no opposition when, three days later, they again crossed the river to bury their dead. Buzzards were circling in the hot summer air as they climbed the hill. When they reached them, the bodies of the slain were unrecognizable. They

had been scalped and mutilated by the Indians, exposed
to the heat, and preyed on by the wolves. The settlers
decided to bury them in a common grave. Daniel was
more fortunate. He found Israel and took him back to
Boone's Station.

The triumph of the Indians was brief. In spite of the
universal sorrow in Kentucky and the fear felt there,
a thousand men under George Rogers Clark gathered
at the mouth of the Licking by the end of September.
Among them were Colonel Logan, John Floyd, and
Daniel. They swept through the forests of Ohio, burning villages, destroying large supplies of grain and dried
meat, and created panic among the Indians.

Something had happened to the tribes Simon had
united and led to a terrible triumph. Their strength had
left them at the very moment of their success. They did
not come out in bands or from their single villages to
face the invading army. They never threatened Kentucky again in large numbers. The beavers, in Simon
Girty's phrase, had been forced to leave their dam.

CHAPTER XX

THE LAND THAT WASN'T HIS

THE BATTLE OF THE BLUE LICKS, FOUGHT AT SUCH terrible cost that summer of 1782, was the turning point both for Daniel and the Kentucky he had done so much to explore and open for settlement.

The battle did not put an immediate end to Indian raiding parties. These were to cross the Ohio, stealing horses, snatching occasional scalps, and killing lonely families for the next thirteen years until General Wayne, known because of his boldness as "Mad Anthony," conquered all the tribes to the north.

As late as 1792, when Kentucky separated from Virginia to form the fifteenth state, there were still enough red men around for Isaac Shelby, the first governor, to claim that Kentucky remained "a frontier infested with a savage foe."

Even so, the battle of the Blue Licks brought about a change. In its way it was a victory in spite of being a tragic and unnecessary defeat. After it no large Indian force invaded Kentucky again. The war parties which

149

did come came only occasionally and were small. The
old dread was gone and so, to a great extent, was the old
fear. To men and women who had survived the earlier
dangers, the peace they had dreamed of before the "year
of blood" now seemed at hand.

Instead of making life comfortable for Daniel, peace
presented him with a different kind of danger. It created
problems he had never known and was not ready to face.
He did not understand peace and, as the years went by,
he found it hard to adjust himself to the new Kentucky
which he had helped make possible.

After that awful summer of 1782 Daniel had every
reason to believe life would be a little easier for him.
He was a hero on the frontier, so famous that his name
was becoming known in Europe. Travelers journeyed
far to see him. Young people wanted to hear the celebrated pioneer, nearing fifty, tell his tales of the wild old
times. In more ways than one it looked as if the dangers
and hardships which Daniel had long endured were
finally to bring him his deserved rewards.

Daniel was now a rich man. His hard battle against
poverty seemed to be won. He owned a lot of land in
Kentucky. At any rate he thought he did. Was it fifty
thousand acres? Or a hundred thousand? He wasn't
sure. He did know, however, as his neighbors knew, that
land was money. He made even more money by hunting
and trading, and by being a surveyor who was always
busy.

But the good days, the happy days, the days of being

treated like a hero and knowing the pleasures of prosperity, were soon over. Daniel could never quite understand why or how they ended as they did. Yet, little by little, in ways which confused him, he discovered that instead of being rich he was once again poor—indeed, poorer than he had ever been before.

Daniel was a man made to live close to nature rather than to men. He was a giant in the forest who proved to be a babe when he got out of the woods. Being himself honest, he assumed everyone else was honest, too. He neither liked nor could learn the ways and values of civilization.

There was the matter of land. Land to be tramped over, land to hunt on, the beauty of great forests, or open valleys, green and rolling—these Daniel understood. No one knew them better or loved them more than he. But land as something controlled by law; land as private property instead of a wilderness; land to be bought and sold and fenced in; land, in short, as what he described as a "Bissness," he did not understand.

He had no interest in legal details and was as poor at business as he was at spelling. He was simple enough to believe that the mere act of getting somewhere first, and fighting for what one had explored or settled, was enough to establish ownership. Moreover, he was so busy surveying for other people that he had hardly any time to look after his own affairs.

Daniel was not the only pioneer in Kentucky to find himself ousted by newcomers from acres which he had cleared and fought for. These newcomers were men who had done nothing about the property they took possession of except to get a legal title to it in far-off and safe Virginia. Daniel's losses proved to be double. Bit by bit, because his claims had been carelessly made, his land was taken from him. Worse still, having guaranteed to get clear titles to the lands he surveyed for others, he had to pay large sums to his employers when these titles proved faulty, as they did again and again.

Occasionally, dangers of the old kind presented themselves in the old way. To Daniel such dangers were almost welcome. They were trials he knew how to handle. For instance, there was the day he was working in the shed where his dried tobacco was hanging. He was standing on a platform high above the ground when he looked down to find himself surrounded by four Shawnee braves.

"Now, Boone," their leader said, smiling, "we got you. We carry you off to Chillicothe this time. You no cheat us any more."

Daniel was far away from his cabin and unarmed. He recognized the warriors as men he had known during his captivity and gave them a warm welcome. They commanded him to come down and surrender at once. Daniel assured them that he looked forward to being back in Chillicothe again but asked them, as his blood brothers, please to let him finish his job of rehanging the tobacco.

Although they knew him too well not to be suspicious,

Daniel threw an armful of dried tobacco down
on the Indians

Daniel quieted their doubts by asking questions about old Shawnee friends. The four braves watched him with upturned faces as he worked and talked. Just when they thought he was ready to give himself up, Daniel threw an armful of the dried tobacco down on them, blinding them with the dust, and made a quick dash for his cabin and rifle. After they had stopped coughing and wiping their eyes, the Indians were too wise to follow him. Instead, they crept away into the woods, angry with Daniel for his trickery and with themselves for having been deceived by it.

C H A P T E R   X X I

H E R O ' S   D E P A R T U R E

DANIEL WAS NOW TO FACE A NEW KIND OF FOE, ONE against which he was helpless. He became involved in a long, dull series of legal battles. These skirmishes soon persuaded him that, though fighting Indians was bad enough, fighting in the law courts was much worse.

Every time Daniel was called into a courtroom as a witness he had to testify not only *for* one person but *against* another. The losers blamed him for their losses and became his enemies. And the number of his enemies began to grow until there were many who hated him as much as they had once admired him.

Daniel became increasingly unhappy. Bad luck dogged him. His affairs were made the more muddled when John Floyd was killed by Indians and his papers were lost. Floyd was a friend who was helping him in his legal struggles. Among the papers lost were many Daniel was depending on to prove his rights.

Other blows fell just as hard, if not harder. Daniel was hurt when, within three short summers after the battle of the Blue Licks, he was told that even Boone's

Station, which he had settled, defended and expanded,
no longer belonged to him and his family. Although lawyers could explain to judges why such decisions were
just, they could not explain them to Daniel. He could
not understand why Kentucky, his "Promised Land,"
had become for him a land of broken promises.

He had always needed money and seldom had any.
Now he needed it more than he ever needed it in the
past. While he was struggling in the law courts and losing not only his lands but his hopes of prosperity, Daniel
tried several jobs and was constantly on the move. He
turned tavern- and store-keeper for a while. He took up
farming. He served as a member of the Legislature,
guided immigrants, labored as a surveyor, and did some
horse trading.

For some years Daniel lived in Kanawha County,
Virginia (today West Virginia), where he had at least
the pleasure of being made a lieutenant-colonel in the
militia. Then he returned to Kentucky and built a cabin
on his son's land.

There, though the present was empty, the past he had
made glorious was all around him. The Blue Licks was
only twelve miles away. Boonesborough and Boone's
Station were not far distant. The Warriors' Path was
nearby. So was the place where he had saved Jemima
and the Calloway girls from their Indian kidnappers
and the place where later on he had himself been made
a captive by the Shawnees.

Daniel was not a man to live on memories. His heart

was heavy; the new troubles he faced began to bring out his old restlessness. He resented the newcomers who were building close to him and destroying the game. He longed to be again on a real frontier. He was older now and, like many another pioneer, he suffered from rheumatism. He suffered so much that, when he went hunting, Rebecca often had to carry his rifle for him.

He remained a superb shot. "I am no Statesman I am a Woodsman," he wrote to the governor. And one of the greatest of woodsmen he continued to be. In spite of his age, his eyes were clear, his face lean, his hair still reddish, his skin remarkably fair, his shoulders square, and his spirit aching for adventure.

Tempting stories began to reach him about Missouri, which was then Spanish-owned. It was sparsely settled. There was an abundance of game. The country was fertile, and pioneers were needed. Just as Daniel's grandfather had sent his children over from England to report on Pennsylvania, so Daniel had his son, Daniel Morgan Boone, go ahead to look over Missouri.

When the young man returned, Daniel must have thought he was listening to John Finley once again. The new country was everything rumor had said it was. Better still, the Spanish lieutenant-governor would be honored to have Boone settle there. He went so far as to write Daniel a letter, offering him a large land grant for himself, smaller tracts for such families as he might bring along, and further grants of forty acres for each wife, child, or servant.

Daniel was reluctant to leave Kentucky—his Kentucky. After all, he had come there first when he was thirty-five and now he was sixty-five. Kentucky had been his life. He had given much and lost more, and been a leader among those who made it possible for others to live there. Daniel also hated to give up his American citizenship and become a Spanish subject. But he could not resist the Spanish government's offer.

Kentucky had treated Daniel with strange indifference. In 1796 it had refused his request to help mark and cut a new road that was being built. It had even forgotten to pay him for his important share in opening the Wilderness Road 'way back in '75. To be sure, the year before Daniel had his letter from the Spanish lieutenant-governor, Kentucky had named a new county after him. This was nice, very nice, and would have been nicer if during the same year two other counties had not sold more than ten thousand acres of Daniel's land in Kentucky because he could not pay the taxes.

Daniel made up his mind to accept Spain's generosity and move to Missouri. Rebecca, dauntless as always though now approaching sixty, was willing to follow him. So were his sons and some of his old friends.

When the news spread in the summer of 1799 that Daniel was to leave in September, Kentuckians suddenly sensed what they were losing. Those who had attacked him forgave him. Those who had ignored him wanted to see him. They all knew, his friends and enemies alike, that this man who was leaving them stood

for their history. He represented their dangers, their
trials, their tragedies and hopes.

As usual, Daniel made his plans carefully. From a
giant tulip poplar on the bank of the Big Sandy he
fashioned a dugout sixty feet long that could carry five
tons. In this canoe Rebecca, some of his family, and
most of his belongings were to travel down the Ohio.

As for himself, he apparently went overland, accompanied by some friends and driving his cattle before
him. His exact route is not known. We do know that
before the Boones and their party left many old friends

and new admirers came to see Daniel off. They came by canoe or on horseback to pay him their respects, and they came in large numbers.

Daniel's whole trip through Kentucky was in the nature of a triumph. People clustered around him, wherever he appeared, to give him their thanks. He was a hero again and left as the hero he had always been. Somewhere on the way he was asked why, at his age, he was leaving land that he had helped to settle. His reply was the well-known "Too many people! Too crowded! Too crowded! I want more elbowroom!"

Elbowroom was what he had always wanted and needed. Elbowroom was what he was now seeking once again.

CHAPTER XXII

A NEW LIFE
AND OLD TROUBLES

THE NEW LIFE IN THE NEW COUNTRY BEGAN BRIGHTLY
for Daniel. It was October when he, his family, and
friends reached St. Louis by land and river. The welcome he was given in this little Missouri town, then the
capital of the Spanish province of Upper Louisiana, was
a warm one. His coming was a public event. He was received by the Spaniards in a way they thought worthy
of a lieutenant-colonel and a famous figure. Flags, Spanish and American, fluttered in his honor and soldiers,
smartly outfitted, paraded for the old man dressed in
the untidy leather clothes of a hunter.

At last, at last, he must have thought, everything is
going to be all right. He had land, and plenty of it. So
did his sons. The land the Boones chose was on Femme
Osage Creek six miles from where it flows into the
Missouri River and some sixty miles west of St. Louis.

It was wild land, almost undisturbed by man. It was
the kind of frontier land that Daniel loved and needed,
had known and was always longing for. It was a hunt-

161

er's paradise where game was plentiful and solitude possible. Best of all, it was *his* land—his and his sons'. The lieutenant-governor had said so and meant what he said. Daniel had papers to prove it. The largest tract—8,500 acres—quite rightly belonged to him. But his children and his friends were also well taken care of.

The Spaniards had lived up to their promises. Having promises kept and dreams realized was for Daniel a new and agreeable experience. Moreover, the Spanish officials respected him so much that, before a year had passed, Daniel himself was made an important Spanish official.

They appointed him "syndic" or commander of the

Femme Osage District. His duties were many, his powers great. Daniel was a one-man government. He was a military leader, a judge, a distributor of land, and a financial administrator all at the same time. He could make what laws he wanted to and punish men as he saw fit.

Wearing his hunting clothes, he held court under a tree—the "Justice Tree"—near his cabin. Since he had his own good and numerous reasons for not liking lawyers or courtrooms, Daniel handled cases in an informal manner that regular judges and lawyers would have frowned on.

He was interested in the truth, not the law; in common sense rather than technicalities. Although strict, he was fair and honest. His neighbors liked his way of doing things. They even forgave him when he sentenced them, as magistrates often did at that time, to lashes "well laid on" their bare backs.

For over four years Daniel enjoyed the pleasures of security. He had property. His family was doing well. He held an important position. He was looked up to. His days were busy and he was happy. He liked his many official duties and, when not performing them, he was off hunting and trapping which he liked even more.

His life seemed at last to be built on a firm foundation. One day that foundation began to crumble. In the new country the old troubles with which he was all too familiar unexpectedly reappeared.

A land deal was made bigger than any Daniel had

ever imagined. It was not a matter of thousands of acres, but of more than a million square miles. Nations and history were involved in it. A wise American President and a cornered European conqueror brought it about. Being the Louisiana Purchase, it had dramatic and far-reaching effects. By a stroke of the pen (a form of pioneering new to Daniel) the size of the United States was doubled in 1803.

The Louisiana Purchase made public the fact that Spain, in a secret treaty three years before, had turned over to France her huge holdings west of the Mississippi. Now France was withdrawing as a power from the continent of North America. And the vast area from Canada to the Gulf of Mexico, which included Missouri and the port of New Orleans, passed overnight into American hands.

The man who engineered this fabulous deal was Thomas Jefferson. The circumstance which made it possible was Napoleon's need for money. Napoleon, by his treaty with Spain, had no right to sell, and Jefferson, under his constitutional powers as President, had no right to buy. But Napoleon had to have funds with which to wage the war with England that he knew was coming.

This gave Jefferson his chance. Acting in the name of the United States on his own responsibility, he bought for a mere fifteen million dollars a territory of a value too great to calculate. His Purchase was one of the wis-

est steps any government ever took. It was the shrewdest of deals, the best of bargains. Its results were stu-
pendous. Yet, along with its superb benefits, one misfor-
tune, however minor, must be mentioned. It brought
ruin once again to Daniel Boone as a landowner.

Had Daniel listened carefully when he first reached
St. Louis, he might have made himself secure. Had politics interested him, he would have taken the needed
precautions. Had decisions made in far-away Madrid,
Paris, or Washington seemed real to him in the wilderness, he would have protected himself. But Daniel made
three serious mistakes as a Spanish subject. These were
to cost him dearly when the United States took possession of Missouri.

He never bothered to send the paper which said the
land was his to be filed in New Orleans. Then, he and
Rebecca, who in their old age wanted to be near their
family, built their cabin on the land of their son Daniel
Morgan Boone, instead of building it on their own land
as they should have done to establish their claim. Finally, Daniel failed to clear each year the number of acres
on his property which the law required. He failed to do
this because he was too busy with his public duties and
because both he and the Spanish lieutenant-governor
believed that as a Spanish official Daniel did not have
to do so.

The American commissioners who looked over Daniel's claim did not want to take his land away from him.

They had to, however. The law was the law to them. Their duty was to see that it was carried out. The result was that Daniel, who had prospered as a Spanish subject and was left undisturbed by the French during their very brief occupation, lost the acres he believed he owned upon finding himself an American again.

His sons were more fortunate. They had cleared their lands; their titles were in good order. For Daniel it was the same old story. Once more what he was sure was safely his had been snatched from him. Whether it was pelts or money, the harvest of a long winter's hunting, or land which his courage and his mastery of the woods had brought him, he was always having them taken away just at the moment when he was certain they would free him from worry.

To lose everything you have struggled to get is hard at any age. At thirty-six it is hard enough. Daniel had learned this a third of a century before when he was robbed by the Indians after those two rugged years in Kentucky. To lose everything at seventy is harder still.

There were certain things no one could take away from Daniel. His character was one of these. His skill as a hunter and his love of the wilderness were others. Daniel was a proud man. Although he was glad to have a rough cabin on his son's property, he liked to be on his own. He needed money to take care of Rebecca and himself. He also had debts in Kentucky which he was determined to pay.

It was only natural that, to support himself, Daniel should turn to the woods where he had always been happiest. Not being a public official any longer, he had plenty of time for hunting and trapping. If, as the years went by, he trapped more than he hunted, it was because his eyes became less clear, his hands less steady, and rheumatism troubled him. Nothing could break his spirit, bend his back, or halt his restless moccasins.

During the summers he worked on the farms belonging to his children or helped his son Nathan with the building of his fine stone house, which is rumored to have taken eight years to finish. When the first promise of cold was in the air and the leaves began to turn, Daniel's heart quickened. The winters brought him freedom. Old as he was, he often struck out for the wilds, there to stay for months at a time. He would camp in the discomfort he found comfortable and tramp for miles through the woods, hunting and trapping, at peace with the world and at peace with himself.

A young Negro was his helper. Occasionally the two of them would have their difficulties with Indians. These dangers amused Daniel. Like the pioneer's life he now relived and the exciting loneliness of unsettled lands which he was once more enjoying, his stray encounters with red men reminded him of the days that had been and rolled the years away.

Daniel is said to have walked at least twice all the way back to Kentucky. Once he went there to pay his debts. When he had paid them, the story goes, he had only fifty cents left. Nonetheless, he went home a happier man. If his pockets were lighter, so was his conscience.

On one of these visits he met, and at once became the friend of, John James Audubon, a young man then unknown who was to become as famous as Daniel himself. He was an excellent shot and loved the out-of-doors with Daniel's passion. Audubon, however, approached nature as an artist, not a hunter. No one knew American wild life better than he, and no one has made finer pictures of its birds and animals.

Daniel liked Audubon so much that he even took him hunting and showed him how to "bark off" a squirrel at fifty paces. "Barking off" was a true test of marksmanship. It meant bagging a squirrel not by hitting him but by hitting the branch just behind him, so that the animal would fall to the earth killed by the shock rather than the bullet.

Daniel thrilled young Audubon with some of his tallest tales. They were stories of all kinds; stories about his escapes from Indians, or his ability to settle a boundary dispute by remembering the exact location of a tree he had marked but had not seen for twenty-five years.

One night after their return from the hunt, when Audubon and Daniel shared a room, they continued to talk for long hours about many things. When at last they were talked out and ready for sleep, Daniel showed

how little he cared about the comforts of civilization.
He refused the bed offered him, slipped off his hunting
shirt, wrapped some blankets around him, and lay down
to rest on the floor as if it were the ground and he were
out camping.

CHAPTER XXIII

HEADING WEST

ALTHOUGH LITTLE BY LITTLE AGE WAS OVERTAKING Daniel, he did not seem to realize it. He was stronger than most men, younger in spirit, and could outwalk those not nearly so old as he was. Perhaps he could not shoot quite so well as he used to. Nevertheless he could still handle a rifle as few could. Of course, his rheumatism sometimes caused him pain. Not much. At least not too much. He felt fine. He could hold his own with anyone.

Accordingly, when the War of 1812 broke out, he hurried off at once and volunteered. But his services were refused. Daniel could not understand why. After all, he was only seventy-eight. He knew more about frontier warfare than all these young fellows who were accepted could ever hope to know. Furthermore, he did not like the idea of his sons' doing his fighting for him. As it turned out, the government could not keep Daniel entirely out of the war. When it reached Missouri in terms of occasional Indian raids inspired by the English,

Daniel is reported to have taken part in a skirmish
fought on the property of one of his relatives.

In March, 1813, Rebecca died. She was seventy-three
and hers had been a hard life, filled like Daniel's with
trials and dangers. She had lived it courageously and
without complaints, always ready to follow her husband
into the wilderness, always equal to the harsh demands
of the frontier. Her death exposed Daniel to a new kind
of loneliness.

Daniel mourned Rebecca sincerely. Already poor, he
was much poorer when she died. He abandoned their
cabin and at his sons' request made his home with them.
Within a year of Rebecca's going some news reached
Daniel which he would have liked to share with her.
The two of them had waited for it a long time. The
Congress of the United States, due to the activity of
some of Daniel's loyal friends in Kentucky, had finally
passed a bill granting some land in Missouri to Daniel
in recognition of his services to the nation.

It was not as much land as had been taken away from
him by the American commissioners. Daniel had asked
for 8,500 acres, which was what the Spaniards had
given him. At the last moment, however, someone in
Washington for no good reason whittled the grant down
to 850 acres.

Considering what Daniel had done, this was a
wretched reward and, quite rightly, it made him mad.
Even so, it was something. Or rather it would have
been, had not two or three Kentuckians who still had

claims against the old man heard about the grant and
rushed to Missouri to collect what he owed them. Daniel, being Daniel, paid them off by selling the land his
grateful government had awarded him.

Although at first angry, his anger soon cooled. It
pleased him to know that his country had not forgotten
him entirely. As for land, *his own land,* it would have
been nice to have it. But since his sons had plenty,
Daniel no longer really cared about owning any.

The land he loved was still his. This was the land
where there were few, if any, settlers; the land that no
one had claimed; the land that remained wild. Game
was as numerous as it had been many years ago in the
Yadkin Valley, in Kentucky when he first came there,
and on his arrival in the Femme Osage district.

As always, he was drawn to the West. He had heard
about mountains there higher than any he had ever
crossed and a beautiful country filled with strange sights
he was anxious to see. He had been told he could find
salt, valuable salt, and a lot of it. He had listened to
stories about the great plains east of the Rockies which
were suddenly darkened by huge herds of buffalo.

These were tales Daniel could not resist and, because
of them, the old wanderer continued to wander. Places
six hundred miles distant did not seem far away to him.
Exactly where he went before or after Rebecca's death
is not known, though after she died his journeys probably grew longer. It is known that he trapped all over
Missouri; that when he was eighty-two he was seen

near the present site of Kansas City; and that he did
reach the Platte River.

It is also known that he was always asking questions
about California, and that at eighty-four he made
definite plans to visit the "salt mountains" with "three
whites and a party of Osage Indians." There are those
who say that he even got as far as the Rockies and visited the Yellowstone. He probably did. Daniel was that
kind of man.

Even Daniel could not keep on trapping and hunting
forever. In the last two years of his life, when his thick
hair was white and he was a feeble old man, he stayed
close to the homes of his sons and relatives. He was
happy. He liked his children and their families, and
they liked him. He had countless grandchildren who
loved to hear the stories he loved to tell. He had many
friends too, and people made long journeys just to see
and hear him.

Although Daniel still took short trips on foot or on
horseback, he traveled chiefly in his talk. He liked to go
back in time and to share the excitements of other days
and places with those who came to see him. One of
these was an artist, Chester Harding, who painted his
portrait. He found Daniel living alone in a cabin and
roasting a steak of venison on the end of his ramrod.

While Harding was painting, Daniel told him about
one of his early hunting trips. When Harding learned
that Daniel never carried a compass, he asked if he had
ever been lost in the woods. "No," Daniel replied, "I

can't say as ever I was lost, but I was *bewildered* once
for three days."

The unknown had never frightened Daniel. As death
came nearer, he was no more afraid of it than he had
been of life. He made his plans for it as carefully as he
had for any of his other expeditions. He had a carpenter
make him a black walnut coffin which, to the horror of
his grandchildren, he kept in his cabin. When a friend
died unexpectedly, he gave this one away, having discovered by trying it out that it was too small for him

anyway. Then he bought another coffin, made this time of cherry wood.

Daniel died almost without suffering on the 26th of September, 1820. He had been taken sick very suddenly a few days before, while staying with a son-in-law. A doctor urged him to remain quiet but Daniel paid no attention.

As soon as he felt better, he insisted upon riding his horse to the home of his son Nathan. There he died three days later, in the stone house he had helped to build. He was buried, as he wanted to be, in the cherry-wood coffin, next to Rebecca in a mound about a mile from the Missouri River.

That Daniel was ready to go is shown by a letter he wrote to his sister-in-law four years before. It is a re-markable and moving letter. Its bad spelling in its original form (see below*) cannot hide the fact that an uncommonly good man wrote it. No better portrait of Daniel Boone exists.

* "Deer Sister
"With pleasuer I Rad a Later from your sun Samuel Boone who informs me that you are yett Liveing and in good health Considering your age I wright to you to Latt you know I have Not forgot you and to inform you of my own Situation sence the Death of your Sister Rabacah I Leve with flanders Calaway But am at present at my sun Nathans and in tolarabel halth you Can gass at my feilings by your own as we are So Near one age I Need Not write you of our satuation as Samuel Bradley or James grimes Can inform you of Every Surcomstance Relating to our famaly and how we Leve in this World and what Chance we shall have in the next we know Not for my part I am as ignerant as a Child all the Relegan I have to Love and fear god beleve in Jeses Christ Don all the good to my Nighbour and my self that I Can and Do as Little harm as I Can help and trust on gods marcy for the Rest and I Beleve god neve made a man of my prisepel to be Lost and I flater my self Deer sister that you are well on your way in Cristeanaty gave my Love to all your Childran and all my frends fearwell my Deer sister
                                   "Daniel Boone"

"Dear Sister," he wrote, "With pleasure I read a letter from your son Samuel Boone who informs me that you are yet living and in good health, considering your age. I write to you to let you know I have not forgot you and to inform you of my own situation. Since the death of your sister Rebecca I live with Flanders Calloway but am at present at my son Nathan's and in tolerable health. You can guess at my feelings by your own as we are so near one age. I need not write you of our situation as Samuel Bradley or James Grimes can inform you of every circumstance relating to our family and how we live in this world and what chance we shall have in the next we know not. For my part I am as ignorant as a child.

"All the religion I have is to love and fear God, believe in Jesus Christ, do all the good to my neighbor and myself that I can, and do as little harm as I can help, and trust on God's mercy for the rest, and I believe God never made a man of my principle to be lost. And I flatter myself, dear sister, that you are well on your way in Christianity. Give my love to all your children and all my friends. Farewell, my dear sister. Daniel Boone."

Even death did not put an end to the wanderings of Daniel and Rebecca. Twenty-five years after Daniel died the State of Kentucky persuaded the State of Missouri that the Boones belonged in Kentucky. The Kentucky officials promised to build a monument in Frankfort worthy of the man and woman whose graves it was to mark.

A great procession, a great crowd, an eloquent oration, and military honors welcomed Daniel and Rebecca back. But, though Kentucky was proud of the Boones and proud to have them Kentuckians once again, the promised monument was not built for another thirty-five years. Their real monument, however, was too large for any cemetery to hold. It was the new country in the wilderness which they had helped to explore and settle.

INDEX

178